IMAGES
of America
LOST DENVER

DEMOLITION PROTEST, 1990. When the elegant Jules Jacques Benoit Benedict–designed Central Bank and Trust Company faced demolition (see page 66), historical preservationists rallied, unsuccessfully, to save the building. These protesters carry signs with a vintage photograph of the building (by Louis Charles McClure, an important early 20th-century Denver photographer), a testament to the importance of historic images to an appreciation of Denver's history. (Roger Whitacre collection.)

ON THE COVER: MAY-D&F, 1965: The pride of downtown, the glass-walled concrete hyperbolic paraboloid structure in front of the May-D&F department store became an instant landmark when it opened in 1958. Here, it backdrops a lunchtime concert by the North High School Concert Band. It was demolished in 1996, despite many Denver citizens' hopes for its preservation. (Denver Public Library, Western History Collection.)

IMAGES
of America
LOST DENVER

Mark A. Barnhouse

ARCADIA
PUBLISHING

Published by Arcadia Publishing
Charleston, South Carolina

Library of Congress Control Number: 2015941077

For all general information, please contact Arcadia Publishing:
Telephone 843-853-2070
Fax 843-853-0044
E-mail sales@arcadiapublishing.com
For customer service and orders:
Toll-Free 1-888-313-2665

Visit us on the Internet at www.arcadiapublishing.com

To Matt Wallington, who helps me remember

INTRODUCTION

Denver, the Mile High City, has existed only since 1858, making it younger than most other American cities of comparable size. Its economy has cycled through numerous booms and busts. During booms, each new generation of city builders has sought to make its mark, assuming its works would endure for decades, if not centuries. Each subsequent generation, however, has wiped away, in some later boom, the legacy of those who came before, in the never-ending quest to remake the city.

Some changes have been natural, even necessary. If they are to thrive, cities must evolve as they attract new residents and new technologies develop. Certainly, no Denverite would want to return to unpaved manure-filled streets, nor would any sensible person want to preserve in amber every unpleasant aspect of today's Denver. But likewise, no thoughtful resident would want to erase the past entirely in favor of a Denver filled only with generic new buildings, no different from anyplace else.

The idea that we might want to preserve some important pieces of our past is not new. Denver's first historical preservationist was Margaret Tobin Brown (known posthumously, but never while she was living, as Molly Brown). In 1927, when the former home of Denver journalist and poet Eugene Field was threatened with demolition, she bought it, and later paid to move it to Washington Park, where it stands today. In 1932–1933, architect Jules Jacques Benoit Benedict sought ways to adaptively reuse the old Denver County Courthouse, a grand, if outgrown, 1883 edifice occupying a full block downtown at Sixteenth Street and Court Place. He proposed a museum, a permanent exhibition of Colorado products, and other functions. It was to no avail; the penny-pinching administration of Mayor George Begole, having just moved into the then new city and county building, wanted the courthouse either sold or demolished. Since there were no buyers with that much ready money during the Great Depression, down it came.

Then came World War II, followed by a new generation of city builders, encouraged by youthful mayor James Quigg Newton. Anxious to cement Denver's status as an important city, these men (and they were *all* men) sold key downtown landmarks to any developer willing to give the city a dynamic, modern skyline. On Capitol Hill and in other historic neighborhoods, developers razed mansions built by 19th-century gold and silver barons, often replacing them with parking lots or cheaply built apartments. Following the lead of other cities, Denver created the Denver Urban Renewal Authority (DURA), which facilitated new opportunities for private developers downtown, and which, ignoring the wishes of many of their residents, rid the city of whole neighborhoods it deemed "blighted slums" (what was then called Lower Downtown, centered on Larimer, Lawrence and Arapahoe Streets, and Auraria, just southwest of downtown, being the most prominent examples). A great many people at the time approved of DURA's efforts; at the urging of Mayor Thomas Currigan, Denver voters handily passed DURA's Skyline/Lower Downtown renewal plan in 1967.

Some did not approve. Modern-day historic preservation in Denver was born in the 1960s, as thoughtful residents feared that too much was being lost, and future generations would lack a connection with the city's past. The city-chartered Denver Landmarks Commission was formed in 1967 and initially led by Helen Millett Arndt; she and the commission immediately got to work, attempting, mostly unsuccessfully, to convince DURA not to tear down key buildings in its Skyline project area. About the same time, and for a similar reason, a savvy woman named Dana Crawford formed a partnership to purchase most of the buildings on the 1400 block of Larimer Street and convinced DURA to leave them standing; the result was Larimer Square, today a popular dining and shopping destination. Then, galvanized by the destruction of so many irreplaceable historic buildings, the nonprofit foundation Historic Denver, Inc. was born in 1970. Its first major project was the purchase, renovation, and opening as a museum the then threatened home of Denver's first preservationist, Molly Brown. In the years since, it has pursued other projects, pioneered the use of easements to give old buildings second lives, and continued to advocate for endangered historic structures all over the city.

The story of Lost Denver is told in five chapters. Chapter 1, "Industry and Infrastructure," explores some of the less glamorous aspects of Denver's past; it also takes up the theme of transportation, which has always been key to Denver's economic health and development, and the manufacture and distribution of food. Chapter 2, "Hub of the Rocky Mountain Empire," describes how Denver became the "capital city" of a multistate region, providing goods and services to smaller cities and towns across a vast area. Under post–World War II editor Palmer Hoyt, the *Denver Post* coined the slogan "Voice of the Rocky Mountain Empire," capitalizing on this idea.

Chapter 3, "Urban Removal," focuses on the two DURA projects mentioned above. The 27-block Skyline Project radically changed downtown. To supporters, it succeeded in ridding the city of its skid row and created a collection of shiny high-rise towers that generated higher property taxes than the dilapidated buildings they replaced. To detractors, then and now, Skyline represents a lost opportunity to create a vibrant mix of old and new without sacrificing human scale and history, as the completed Skyline has done; skid row is not gone, it has merely relocated. Auraria, just southwest of downtown, was a mixed neighborhood of residents, small businesses, and industry. DURA demolished most of it for the Auraria Higher Education Center, leaving a few isolated historic buildings devoid of context. While countless thousands have benefitted from this centrally located campus, memories of former residents are long.

Chapter 4, "Amusements," describes how Denverites have spent their leisure hours, in theaters, restaurants, amusement parks, sports venues, and concert halls. Chapter 5, "Only Yesterday," highlights landmarks from the second half of the 20th century that lived too-brief lives before disappearing, as the cycle of build, use, then demolish, accelerated in recent years. By the 1990s, it became apparent to preservationists that they should broaden the definition of historic to include architecturally significant works from even the recent past.

Lost Denver is about more than buildings, regardless of how important its remaining historic fabric is to Denver's continuing economic vitality. Cities are more than buildings—everyday lives of citizens deserve chronicling just as much as landmarks. Amusements, restaurants, hotels, factories, newspapers, and stores are gone, but not forgotten, in these pages. Chronicling them is not mere nostalgia if it places them in the context of the evolving story of a vibrant city.

In the 21st century, when Denver has again become the destination for thousands of newcomers, it is important to reflect on various Denvers that have come before. Had Leo Tolstoy been an urbanist, he might have written, "Mediocre cities are all alike, but each great city is great in its own way." For Denver to continue to be the great city it has long been, Denverites must engage with their city's past even as they continue to create the future Denver, the great city that its people have always imagined to be coming but that has actually always been present all around them.

One

INDUSTRY AND INFRASTRUCTURE

NATIONAL MINING AND INDUSTRIAL EXPOSITION, 1882. This *Harper's Weekly* illustration shows a 150,000-square-foot building on Broadway and Exposition Avenue that briefly showcased Colorado's mineral riches. Architect Willoughby J. Edbrooke worked for a committee headed by millionaire Horace Tabor. Reached via Tabor's and William Loveland's Circle Line Railway, the exposition, meant to be permanent, ran for three summers only, and the building was demolished soon after. (DPL, Z-4064.)

ARGO SMELTER EMPLOYEES, C. 1890. Initially operating in Black Hawk, Colorado, the Argo Smelter of Nathaniel P. Hill's Boston and Colorado Company moved to a Denver site between Broadway and Pecos Street and Forty-fourth and Forty-eighth Avenues (today's names) in 1878. It formed the nucleus of a worker's village, largely populated by Swedish, German, and Slavic immigrants. The smelter burned down in 1913 and did not reopen. (HC, 10049315.)

OMAHA AND GRANT SMELTER, C. 1892. Not far from Argo, on the east bank of the South Platte River, the Omaha and Grant Smelter opened in 1883 after James B. Grant, who had formerly operated in Leadville, Colorado, merged his operation with the Omaha Smelter Company. Processing gold, silver, lead, and copper, it was later part of an 1899 merger that formed the American Smelting and Refining Company (ASARCO). (Author's collection.)

SMOKESTACK DEMOLITION, 1950. Built in 199 days in 1892, the Omaha and Grant smokestack was imploded (right) at 4:58 p.m. on Saturday, February 25, 1950, in one of the most-watched demolitions in Denver history. After the smelter closed in 1902, the property sat vacant, the buildings eventually demolished, but the 352-foot brick smokestack remained a landmark on the skyline for decades. One reuse proposal included turning it into an observation tower, but by 1950 the stack was determined to be unsafe after cracks formed. Perhaps sensing the symbolism of the moment, as Denver's dirty industrial past gave way to a future that people hoped would be cleaner, thousands turned out, parking in the lot of the then under-construction Denver Coliseum and watching from every angle (below). (Both, HC, right, 10043993, below, 10043994.)

GLOBE SMELTER, C. 1900. The third of Denver's smelters was the Globe, near Fifty-first Avenue and Pearl Street. Owned by Denverite Dennis Sheedy for some years, it later became part of ASARCO, specializing in highly toxic cadmium smelting, until closing in 2006. In early years, its workforce was predominantly Eastern European, and even today the adjacent Globeville neighborhood is home to St. Joseph's Polish Parish. (Author's collection.)

SOUTH BROADWAY, C. 1940. Three industries clustered near Broadway and Mississippi Avenue in the early 20th century. Gates Rubber built its plant west of Broadway in 1914 (center); Ford Motor Company opened an automobile factory (center right) in 1913; and Shwayder Trunk Company (later Samsonite) manufactured luggage here from 1923 until 1966 (bottom right). All but the Ford building (now offices) are gone; Gates was demolished in 2014. (HC, 10043985.)

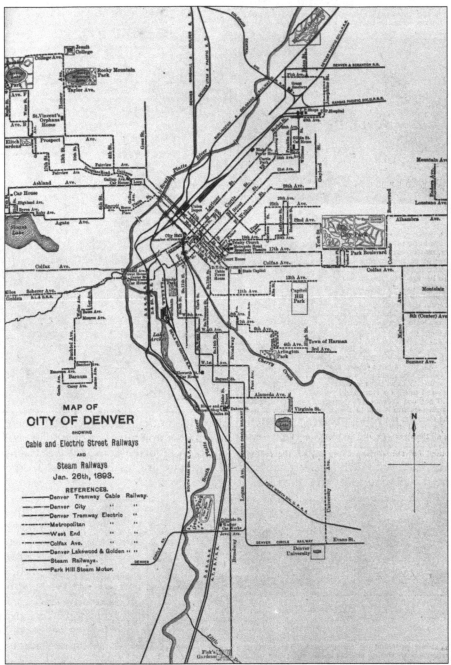

STREET RAILWAYS MAP, 1893. Denver once enjoyed one of the most extensive and efficient streetcar systems for a city of its size in the United States. In 1899, the Denver City Tramway Company (later Denver Tramway Corporation) was formed when several lines consolidated; the company built additional lines and extensions in the early 20th century. Rail lines eventually gave way to trolley coaches (rubber-tired buses powered by overhead electrical lines), and then diesel buses, with the last few streetcars making their final runs on June 3, 1950. Denver Tramway Corporation eventually went bankrupt and was superseded by today's Regional Transportation District (RTD). (HC, 10043986.)

WELCOME ARCH, 1906. Greeting arrivals at Union Station from 1906 until 1931, when Mayor George Begole ordered it removed as a traffic hazard, this iron arch with 1,600 lightbulbs was designed by East High School student Mary Woodsen. In 1908, the word *Mizpah*, a Hebrew term meaning "the Lord watch between me and thee, when we are absent from one another," was added to this Seventeenth Street face. (HC, 10026583.)

RAIL YARDS, 1909. The land behind Union Station, viewed here from the Sixteenth Street viaduct, was filled, until the late 1980s, with extensive trackage for the railroad companies. It was these tracks that made nine viaducts necessary, all now gone or replaced. Today, a consolidated main line runs through a portion of this site, with the rest platted with new streets and filled with residential and commercial buildings. (*DMF.*)

SIXTEENTH STREET VIADUCT, C. 1905. Rail yards prevented residents of North Denver and the then independent town of Highlands from easily reaching downtown. Sixteenth Street merchants agitated for a solution, so the Denver City Cable Railway built this wooden viaduct in 1889, complete with a transfer point to Union Station (right), reached via stairs. The viaduct was rebuilt in 1924; the replacement in turn was demolished in 1993. (DPL, X-18333.)

FIFTEENTH STREET, C. 1908. Although not readily apparent today, in its time Fifteenth Street was as important to downtown Denver as Sixteenth and Seventeenth Streets. Thanks to extensive streetcar service, a legacy of competition before the 1899 streetcar consolidation, Fifteenth Street developed into a street lined with restaurants, numerous shops, and a concentration of grocers, complete with its own merchants association and landmarks. (HC, 10034175.)

TRAMWAY CENTRAL LOOP, C. 1912 (ABOVE) AND C. 1905 (BELOW). As a convenient central transfer point, Denver Tramway Company built the central loop off of Fifteenth Street between Arapahoe and Lawrence Streets (above, viewed from the Daniels and Fisher Tower; below, looking toward Fifteenth Street). The Denver Interurban Railroad (later absorbed by Denver Tramway) built the adjoining interurban loop, connecting Arapahoe and Curtis Streets mid-block between Fifteenth and Fourteenth Streets. Multiple streetcar lines converged here, and from this point passengers could take interurban lines to Golden, Lakewood, Arvada, or Boulder. To take advantage of the traffic, service businesses and grocers clustered around the two loops. After the streetcars and interurban lines stopped running, the central loop was converted to a drive-through banking facility (see page 67). (Both, DPL, above, X-23220, below, X-18327.)

AIRPLANE VIEW, 1923. By the 1920s, Denver's leaders were increasingly focused on ways to facilitate automobile traffic with better viaducts and new roads (the Sixteenth Street replacement viaduct is under construction, center left). The white dotted line (upper left) represents a proposed extension of Broadway, an idea that three decades after this photograph was taken would result in the Valley Highway (Interstate 25), which partly follows that line. (*DMF.*)

DENVER MOTOR HOTEL, 1930. With the rise of the automobile, by the late 1920s parking downtown was becoming difficult. To solve this problem, Denver's first multilevel purpose-built parking garage arose at 1416 Stout Street in 1928. Designed by George Meredith Musick Sr., with fanciful Art Deco terra-cotta ornamentation, the garage included a gas station and mechanic. It was demolished in 2007, for a hotel. (DPL, X-23832.)

DENVER MUNICIPAL AIRPORT, 1934. In 1927, after becoming the best-known aviator in the world, Charles A. Lindbergh barnstormed cities across the country, promoting air travel and encouraging municipalities (including Denver) to build airports. Denver already had several private airfields, and Mayor Benjamin Stapleton decided to push forward with a city facility. Denver Municipal Airport, at East Thirty-second Avenue and Syracuse Street, opened in October 1929. (HC, 10025327.)

STAPLETON FIELD, C. 1948. The airport, initially ridiculed as "Stapleton's Folly" by the *Denver Post*, grew busy in the 1930s, particularly after the Douglas DC-3 made air travel glamorous. Denver enlisted help from the Works Progress Administration to expand, lengthening and widening runways. In 1944, the airport was named for the still-serving mayor who had conceived it. Aurora is the small town in the distance. (Author's collection.)

FRONTIER AIRLINES, C. 1951. Launched by Raymond M. "Pappy" Wilson in 1946 as Monarch Air, Denver's hometown airline took the name Frontier Airlines after merging with two other Western carriers in 1950. Frontier operated until 1986, when it merged with Houston-based Continental Airlines, which had once been headquartered in Denver. The Frontier name was revived by a new carrier in 1994. (Rob Mohr collection.)

STAPLETON INTERNATIONAL AIRPORT, 1971. The age of jet travel forced Denver to bring its airport up to date. A major expansion, adding a semicircular terminal and three concourses with jetways, was completed in 1966, and the main north-south runway was extended across Interstate 70. At the time of this aerial photograph, an additional concourse (D) was under construction; another (E) would be added in 1987. (HC, 10031778.)

AFTER THE BLIZZARD, 1982. By the early 1980s, Frontier was one of three dominant carriers at Stapleton (the others were United and Continental). The Christmas Eve blizzard of 1982 dumped approximately two feet of snow on a city and an airport ill-equipped to cope with it. The terminal and concourses filled with stranded holiday travelers, giving Denver's airport, then the world's fifth-busiest, a poor reputation. (HC, 10043995.)

STAPLETON TERMINAL INTERIOR, 1979. As part of Stapleton's 50th-anniversary celebration, Frontier Airlines put together a historical exhibit (center). However, by the 60th anniversary 10 years later, Denver was already building Stapleton's replacement, Denver International Airport, which opened in 1995. In 2002, the first residents of a new neighborhood built on the old airport's land moved in; today, only the control tower remains on the site. (HC, 10043989.)

DENVER UNION STOCKYARDS, c. 1948. For much of its history, Denver was called, either proudly or derisively, a cowtown. The Denver Union Stockyards, opened in 1886 and eventually covering 105 acres between the Chicago, Burlington & Quincy Railroad tracks and the South Platte River, was the reason. At its peak, approximately 239,500 cattle, 115,700 hogs, and 306,000 sheep were processed annually, with Swift and Armour operating large plants. (Author's collection.)

SIGMAN MEAT GIVEAWAY, 1939. Just before Christmas each year from 1931 through 1940, the *Denver Post* (building at left) and Denver meatpacker Louis K. Sigman partnered to give away over 100,000 pounds of beef to thousands of needy people. Along Champa Street, people waited in line for hours for a 12-pound bag of meat with a roast and some less-expensive cuts suitable for making soup. (HC, 10043992.)

Kuner Pickle Factory, 1910. Founded by John C. Kuner in 1872 and later bought by his brother Max, the Kuner Pickle Company established a brand name still sold in stores today. Its pickle factory at Twenty-second and Blake Streets, where Coors Field is now, is an example of the many food processors and distributors that once lined the streets of the neighborhoods known today as LoDo and Ballpark. (*DMF.*)

Bredan Butter, c. 1924. Designed to look like a European creamery by commercial artist John Ohnimus, Bredan Butter occupied the southwest corner of Broadway and Mississippi Avenue from 1924 until its 1985 demolition. Bredan's owner, Richard Pinkett, invented the pun name "Bredan" (bread and) to go with its chief product, butter. Production ceased in 1978 after a buy-out; the building had a brief afterlife as a nightclub. (DPL, MCC-3624.)

ZANG BREWERY, C. 1912. German immigrant Philip H. Zang bought Rocky Mountain Brewery (founded in 1859 as Colorado's first) in 1871, renamed it for himself, and built it into the state's largest brewery. Zang sold out to English investors in 1889, with his son Adolph remaining as general manager. The brewery, on the South Platte River at Seventh Street, failed during Prohibition; only the brewmaster's house stands today. (Author's collection.)

TIVOLI PACKING ROOM, C. 1950. Although the Tivoli-Union Brewery survives as the Auraria Student Union, the original Tivoli beer has been gone since 1969. In 1866, German immigrant Moritz Sigi began brewing beer on (today's) Tenth Street in Auraria. It became Tivoli under new owner John Good in 1900. The name Tivoli has been revived as a microbrew and now occupies a portion of the old brewery. (HC, 10032892.)

JOHN THOMPSON GROCERY COMPANY, C. 1910. Founded in 1894 on the ground floor of the Normandie apartment building (right) on Fifteenth Street, opposite the Tramway Central Loop, the John Thompson firm claimed by 1927 to be the largest retail grocer between Chicago and the Pacific Ocean. Most of its customers, approximately 7,000 households daily, telephoned in their orders, which were delivered by a fleet of 140 trucks. (DPL, X-25304.)

CITY MARKET, 1912. The notion of locally grown produce is as popular today as ever, and farmers' markets have sprouted across Denver in recent years. An earlier farmers' market, the municipally run City Market on the west bank of Cherry Creek, between Colfax Avenue and Champa Street, operated for four decades after 1899. Its 238 stalls were rented to Colorado farmers, who served both wholesale and retail customers. (DMF.)

DENARGO MARKET, 1939. By the 1930s, City Market was proving inadequate in its congested downtown site. Farmers formed the Growers Public Market Association in 1938 and contracted with the Union Pacific Railroad in a joint venture to build a new market on 60 acres between Twenty-ninth Street, Brighton Boulevard, and the South Platte River, with access to Union Pacific's lines (above). Denargo Market, named for its location midway between downtown Denver and the old Argo smelter, opened in the summer of 1939. At its opening (below), Temple Buell's functional design, housing over 300 market stalls, impressed all as a great improvement over City Market. Denargo Market thrived for a few decades, but the growth of chain supermarkets after World War II led to its decline and eventual closure in 1974. (Both, HC, above, 10037017, below, 10034734.)

HOME PUBLIC MARKET, C. 1934 (ABOVE) AND 1946 (BELOW). From 1920 to 1948, the Home Public Market served a function in Denver not unlike that of the more famous Pike Place Market in Seattle. Filling 78,000 square feet of space at the eastern corner of Fourteenth and California Streets (below), the market's 70 vendors (above) sold every kind of foodstuff, everyday and exotic. The land underneath the market was owned by the Sisters of Loretto, who had opened the first building of St. Mary's Academy on the corner in 1864. In 1948, the *Denver Post* bought the property and an adjacent six-story building for its new home. It had planned to renovate the market building for its printing plant but found it structurally inadequate, necessitating its demolition. (Above, DPL, X-24093; below, Thomas J. Noel collection.)

Two

THE HUB OF THE ROCKY MOUNTAIN EMPIRE

FESTIVAL OF MOUNTAIN AND PLAIN, 1897. Conceived of as a way to get the city out of its financial and emotional doldrums following the Panic of 1893, the annual Festival of Mountain and Plain was held intermittently from 1895 to 1912, in September or October. This Western Mardi Gras, with the silver serpent as its symbol, featured several days of parades, a royal court, and a masked ball. (HC, 10049120.)

CONSTITUTION HALL, 1963. Home to a restaurant equipment dealer in its final decades, this 1865 building at Fifteenth and Blake Streets was the original First National Bank of Denver. The third floor, added in the early 1870s as the Odd Fellows Hall, was where Colorado's constitution was drafted in 1875–1876. In 1977, a terminated employee of the restaurant-supply house destroyed the building by arson. (HC, 10043987.)

COUNTY COURTHOUSE, C. 1894. The great political question of 1880 was where to build the courthouse. Some interests favored sites on Larimer Street and considered this site, at Sixteenth and Tremont Streets, too far away. The Arapahoe (later Denver) County Courthouse, designed by Elijah E. Myers, opened in 1883, with a fourth floor added in 1893. It was demolished in 1933, despite some pleas for its preservation. (Author's collection.)

DENVER CITY HALL, 1909.
Although not especially well loved in its time, Denver's 1883 City Hall (right), between Larimer and Market Streets and Fourteenth Street and Cherry Creek, nevertheless had a certain presence. It was the scene of the 1894 "City Hall War," when Gov. Davis H. Waite called out the Colorado Infantry to forcibly remove the city's corrupt police and fire boards, who had barricaded themselves inside. City government decamped to the City and County Building in 1932, but this building continued to house, for a time, the police and fire departments. In 1946, Lester F. Smith (the author's grandfather) won the contract to demolish the building. The tower's bell remains on-site today as a memorial. Below, Denver's engineering department poses with its surveying tripods and theodolites on the front steps. (Right, author's collection; below, *DMF.*)

DENVER COUNTY JAIL, 1911. Resembling a cathedral more than a place for incarcerating prisoners, the 1891 Arapahoe (later Denver) County Jail occupied most of a full block between Colfax and Fourteenth Avenues, Santa Fe Drive, and Kalamath Street. Located adjacent to the West Side Courthouse, the 350-bed facility was used until 1956, when it was replaced by a new jail on Havana Street. The 1891 structure was demolished in 1963. (*DMF.*)

ROBERT W. SPEER

CANDIDATE FOR MAYOR

HON. R. W. SPEER now stands, as he has for the past four years, for a progressive business administration of this city, allowing every man, woman and child the greatest personal liberty consistent with the welfare of the city at large. He is not an experiment. Any other mayor would be an experiment

WRITE THE WORD *Speer* ON YOUR BALLOT

ROBERT WALTER SPEER, 1908. The boss mayor whose efforts transformed a utilitarian 19th-century frontier town into a "City Beautiful" 20th-century metropolis, Robert Speer was elected in 1904, reelected in 1908, and served again between 1916 and his death in 1918. Although many (particularly the *Denver Post*) thought his plans extravagant, history has vindicated his spending on parks, parkways, playgrounds, and myriad other civic improvements. (Author's collection.)

CHERRY CREEK SKATERS, 1910. Cherry Creek, flood-prone and considered unsightly, was an early priority for Speer. His administration built walls to tame the creek from downtown to Downing Street, along with now demolished dams like this one. In winter, frozen pools behind the dams were used for skating, which Speer's city-funded magazine, *Denver Municipal Facts*, publicized. City council named the creek-side boulevard for Speer in 1910. (*DMF.*)

SUNKEN GARDENS, 1911. As part of his Cherry Creek improvements, Mayor Speer had landscape architect Saco R. DeBoer create Sunken Gardens Park at a former dump site, between Elati Street and Speer Boulevard. The pavilion was reflected in a large pool and illuminated at night. Today, only its concrete base and steps remain, the pool replaced by grass. The state capitol and Evans School are visible in the distance. (DPL, MCC-1944.)

MUNICIPAL AUDITORIUM, 1906 (ABOVE) AND 1908 (BELOW). Completed in time to host the 1908 Democratic National Convention (below), Speer's Municipal Auditorium at Fourteenth Street between Champa and Curtis Streets was still surrounded by residences in 1906 when construction began on the Robert O. Willison–designed building (above). It was conceived as a multipurpose space, and moveable walls allowed the full building to be used for conventions and trade shows or as a smaller auditorium for lectures and concerts—many of which were free to the public, underwritten by the city. In early years, it hosted Denver's first automobile shows, traveling circuses, and Speer's 1918 funeral. Although the exterior walls remain, the interior was gutted in the 1950s to become the Auditorium Theater and gutted again in 2005 to become the Ellie Caulkins Opera House. (Above, DPL, Z-6854; below, author's collection.)

DEMOLISHED FOR CIVIC CENTER, 1912. Speer created a Denver Art Commission, which proposed a grand civic park connecting the capitol with the Denver County Courthouse and lined with public buildings. Voters rejected this vision in 1906, after which Speer's commission engaged sculptor Frederick MacMonnies to create a new plan. MacMonnies envisioned a two-block park running from Broadway west to Bannock Street to face a future new courthouse, and the voters liked it. Speer managed to purchase the necessary properties before leaving office, and his successor, Mayor Henry J. Arnold, completed the demolitions. Park visitors today are unaware of the various residential and commercial buildings that once occupied Civic Center, including this three-story commercial block on the southwest corner of Broadway and Fourteenth Avenue (above) and these row houses on Bannock Street (below). (Both, *DMF.*)

MOUNT CALVARY CEMETERY, C. 1907. Mount Calvary Cemetery (Catholic, foreground) was still accepting bodies, even though the adjacent City Cemetery (nondenominational, background) had been declared parkland in 1890. During Speer's time, Walter Scott Cheesman's family donated $100,000 for a pavilion memorializing him, giving a name to the park. Some Mount Calvary bodies were not removed until the Denver Botanic Gardens took over the site in 1959. (HC, 10032889.)

DENVER POST BUILDING, 1948. The only Denver daily newspaper still publishing as of this writing, the *Denver Post* is not lost, but most of its previous homes are. In 1907, *Post* owners Frederick Gilmer Bonfils and Harry Heye Tammen built 1544 Champa Street, depicted here by artist Herndon Davis. It remained here until 1950, after which the building was demolished for an expansion of the Woolworth's store next door. (Author's collection.)

DENVER POST BUILDING, C. 1950 AND TEMPLE COURT BUILDING, C. 1910. After World War II, new *Denver Post* publisher E. Palmer Hoyt knew that the paper desperately needed a new plant. The 1902 Temple Court Building (below) and the adjoining Home Public Market, located along California Street between Fifteenth and Fourteenth Streets, and conveniently catercorner from the Denver Dry Goods, the paper's largest advertiser, were available. The *Post* bought them and hired Temple Hoyne Buell to design a makeover of Temple Court and a new printing plant in place of the old public market. The paper vacated the property in 1989, and Buell's handsome Art Moderne design was lost when the buildings were demolished in 1998. The site is now home to Denver's largest hotel. (Above, DPL, X-28803; below, Rob Mohr collection.)

CERVI'S JOURNAL, 1957. Eugene Debs Cervi had worked for both the *News* and *Post* when, in 1945, he launched the four-page *Cervi's News Service*, a forum for investigative journalism and liberal political opinion. In 1949, he transformed it into *Cervi's Rocky Mountain Journal*, covering business and politics, often taking the *Post* to task (left). It continues today as the *Denver Business Journal* but without Cervi's crusading journalistic style. (DPL.)

STRAIGHT CREEK JOURNAL, 1976. Medill Barnes's and Morgan Smith's weekly *Straight Creek Journal*, like *Cervi's*, also exposed the doings of Denver's powerful men, along with arts coverage. Published between 1971 and 1981, it often focused on Donald R. Seawell, who was both publisher of the *Denver Post* and head of the Bonfils Foundations, which were promoting construction of the Denver Center for the Performing Arts. (Suzanne Ryan collection.)

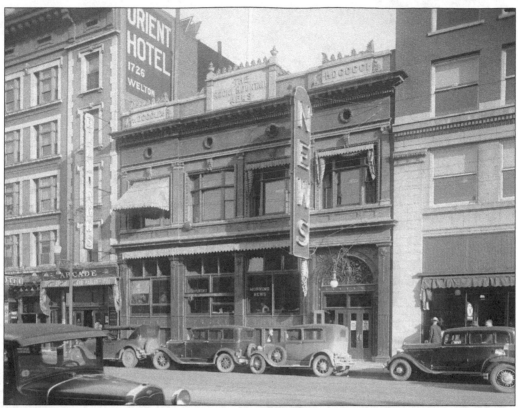

ROCKY MOUNTAIN NEWS BUILDING, C. 1934 (ABOVE) AND C. 1935 (RIGHT). William Newton Byers began publishing Colorado's first newspaper, the *Rocky Mountain News*, on April 19, 1859. When Thomas M. Patterson owned the paper, he moved it to this building at 1720 Welton Street (above), its home from 1901 to 1952. Patterson was the first owner of the *Rocky* to know the wrath of the *Denver Post*'s co-owner Frederick G. Bonfils, even once suffering a physical attack by the rival publisher. Newspaper wars continued under subsequent owners, but one constant was Harry Mellon Rhoads (right), who served from 1900 to 1969, the longest-tenured newspaper photographer in American history. The *News* enjoyed a journalistic renaissance in its final decades, winning multiple Pulitzer Prizes, before it ceased publication on February 27, 2009. (Both, DPL, above, Rh-237, right, Rh-1220.)

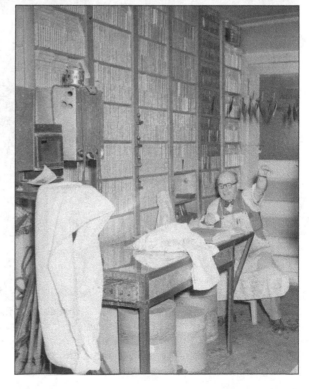

DENVER TRIBUNE BUILDING, 1957. Begun on February 6, 1867, as the *Denver Daily*, the *Denver Tribune* was published by Henry Cordes Brown, who also donated land for the state capitol and later built the Brown Palace Hotel. In 1884, it merged with the *Denver Republican*. Its former quarters on the eastern corner of Sixteenth and Market Streets were nearly ready for demolition when this photograph was taken. (DPL, X-25157.)

EUGENE FIELD COTTAGE, C. 1927. The *Tribune*'s most famous managing editor was humorist and poet Eugene Field, who worked for the paper for two years (1881–1883), before leaving Denver for Chicago, Illinois. When his house at 317 West Colfax Avenue was threatened with demolition, Margaret Tobin Brown bought it and paid for its move to Washington Park in 1930, an early example of historical preservation. (DPL, X-26482.)

DENVER REPUBLICAN BUILDING, c. 1910. Occupying a portion of the Robert S. Roeschlaub–designed Union Block on Sixteenth Street, between Arapahoe and Lawrence Streets, the *Republican* was published by Argo Smelter owner Nathaniel P. Hill and later his son Crawford Hill, whose wife reigned over Denver high society. John Shaffer bought the *Republican* in 1913 and combined it with his recently purchased *Rocky Mountain News* and *Denver Times*. (HC, 20007907.)

BENEVOLENT AND PROTECTIVE ORDER OF ELKS, 1912. Fraternal organizations no longer occupy the central position they once did. One of Denver's most important was Elks Lodge No. 17, grandly dominating the northern corner of Fourteenth and California Streets. Dedicated in 1912, this building served as a meeting place for government leaders and businessmen and hosted William J. "Buffalo Bill" Cody's 1917 funeral. It was demolished in 1974, for parking. (*DMF.*)

1656. The Denver Club, Denver, Colorado.

DENVER CLUB, C. 1900. No other private club expressed the Protestant Denver elite's wealth and power like the Denver Club. Ernest Phillip Varian and Frederick Junius Sterner, heavily influenced by architect Henry Hobson Richardson, designed every aspect of the 1889 polychrome stone building at Seventeenth Street and Glenarm Place, even its locally built furniture. It was demolished in 1953 for another Denver Club, a 21-story office tower. (Rob Mohr collection.)

WALL STREET OF THE ROCKIES, C. 1910. In the 19th century, Seventeenth Street's banks and brokerages became the financial center for a multistate region, giving Denver an economic importance beyond other cities its size. Although three buildings in this view remain—the Equitable and Boston buildings and Magnolia Hotel (center left)—everything else is gone, including the California Building (far left) at California Street, demolished in 1961. (Author's collection.)

McPhee Building, c. 1905. Directly across Seventeenth Street from the Denver Club, this 1889 Frank E. Edbrooke design, featuring a frontal center light well, was built by Charles D. McPhee, who had supplied building materials for a number of early landmarks, including Denver City Hall and the Arapahoe County Courthouse. Later named for a subsequent owner, C.A. Johnson, it was demolished in 1975 for the Anaconda Tower. (Author's collection.)

Patterson Building, c. 1937. Next door to the McPhee Building at Seventeenth and Welton Streets, Richard Crawford Campbell, son-in-law of Sen. Thomas M. Patterson, built this 10-story neoclassical office block in 1924, on the site of Patterson's original 1876 residence. It was demolished in 1975, as part of the same project that brought an end to the McPhee and Continental Oil Buildings. (DPL, X-25115.)

SECURITY BUILDING, 1976. Only 50 feet wide on its California Street side, the William E. and Arthur A. Fisher–designed Security Building arose on the southern corner of Seventeenth and California Streets in 1927. Bosworth, Chanute, Loughridge & Company, its bluestocking brokerage-firm owners, occupied a first-floor suite. It later became Empire Savings's headquarters and was demolished in 1992; the site remains vacant as of this writing. (Roger Whitacre collection.)

VAN SCHAACK AND COMPANY, 1976. Next door to the Security Building on Seventeenth Street, between California and Welton Streets, the Art Moderne headquarters of commercial real estate brokerage Van Schaack and Company, designed by Gordon White and built in 1949, was demolished in 1980 for the Dominion Plaza high-rise. In its final few years, this building was occupied by the brokerage Hanifen, Imhoff & Samford. (Roger Whitacre collection.)

INTERNATIONAL TRUST COMPANY, 1912. For the International Trust Company at the eastern corner of Seventeenth and California Streets, William E. and Arthur A. Fisher designed a white marble neoclassical temple with a 28-foot-high banking room. After the trust company merged with First National Bank in 1958, the building was refaced to match First National's adjacent high-rise tower. It was demolished for a plaza in 1975. (*DMF.*)

CONTINENTAL OIL BUILDING, C. 1930. Denver-based Continental Oil Company (later known as Conoco) hired William Norman Bowman to design its 1926 headquarters building on the western corner of Eighteenth Street and Glenarm Place. Seen here from the Cosmopolitan Hotel at Eighteenth Avenue and Broadway, the building was crowned with a massive neon sign. The Continental Oil Building came down for a parking garage in 1975. (DPL, Rh-114.)

REPUBLIC BUILDING, 1980. The first Denver building with underground parking, the George Meredith Musick Sr.–designed Republic Building towered over Sixteenth Street and Tremont Place from 1926 until 1981. It was built as a medical/dental building, and generations of Denverites rode its elevators to their appointments. Preservationist Roger Oram gathered over 8,000 petition signatures to save it, but Denver's tallest building, the 56-story Republic Plaza, took its place. (Roger Whitacre collection.)

MAJESTIC BUILDING, C. 1915. The location of the Frank E. Edbrooke–designed Majestic Building, fronting on Broadway, Cleveland Place, and Sixteenth Street, gave it unmatched prominence. Begun just prior to the Panic of 1893, it remained unfinished until Dennis Sheedy and Charles B. Kountze bought it in 1898. Favored by law firms, it was also the longtime home of Colorado State Bank. It was demolished in 1977. (DPL, MCC-379.)

WEST COURT HOTEL, 1982. Architect Leonidas D. West built the West Court Hotel at 1415 Glenarm Place in 1912. Its graceful, curving white terra-cotta facade and leaded stained-glass windows with a clinging vine motif lent it an elegant air, even as it transitioned from a tourist hotel into housing for seniors on fixed incomes. Residents in its later years recalled feeling that they were part of a "large family" and enjoyed living downtown. The hotel featured a street-facing courtyard (above). The still-elegant lobby (below) hints at what might have been, had the hotel been saved and renovated. It was demolished in 1982 by a developer who had no specific plans and whose intention of building at the location was stymied by a recession. The site remains a parking lot as of this writing. (Both, Roger Whitacre collection.)

ALBANY HOTEL, C. 1928 (ABOVE) AND C. 1906 (BELOW). The 1885 Albany Hotel, on the eastern corner of Seventeenth and Stout Streets, was one of Denver's important gathering places. Sometimes called "the poor man's Denver Club," the Albany, designed by E.P. Brink, was operated in the beginning by W.H. Cox, who named it for his home city. It was later owned by Thomas B. Patterson and Edward B. Morgan, who made additions in 1906 and 1912 and introduced a live-trout pond in the lobby, from which patrons could catch their dinners. In 1908, the Democrats chose William Jennings Bryan as their presidential candidate in one of the Albany's "smoke-filled rooms." Above, the additions are visible to the left of the original building. Below, diners enjoy the hotel's Bohemian Room restaurant. (Above, DPL, X-29190; below, author's collection.)

NEW ALBANY HOTEL, 1938. In 1937, Patterson's heirs demolished the original building and hired Burnham Hoyt to design a new one to match the height of the earlier additions (below). Hoyt's Art Moderne design, with its high-ceilinged lobby (above), recessed lighting, and heavy use of glass block, featured curves outside and inside, even in the signage. Patterson's heirs sold the hotel in 1950, after which it changed hands every few years. In 1965, James "Jake" Gottlieb, who was associated with the Dunes Resort in Las Vegas, Nevada, and had business ties with Teamsters president James "Jimmy" Hoffa, bought the hotel and spent millions on a renovation that did not respect Hoyt's original design. The hotel closed in 1976 and was demolished in 1977 for a high-rise office building. (Above, DPL, Z-10085; below, author's collection.)

COSMOPOLITAN HOTEL, C. 1957. Incorporating the older, adjacent Hotel Metropole, the 460-room Cosmopolitan, designed by William Bowman, opened at the southeast corner of Broadway and Eighteenth Avenue in 1926. In 1953, Western Hotels of Seattle took over management, giving it a modern makeover that included a new lobby (below), blocking in the ground-floor windows (left), and opening the Outrigger Room, part of the Trader Vic's chain. Western had expansion plans but never acted on them, and there were other expansion plans in later years. A new owner renamed it Plaza Cosmopolitan in 1979 but could not compete with newer downtown hotels. On December 31, 1982, a "Last Night at the Cosmopolitan" was held for 2,000 guests, and the building was imploded in 1984. The site remained a parking lot until 2015. (Left, HC, 10030748; below, Rob Mohr collection.)

PARK LANE HOTEL, C. 1960 (ABOVE) AND C. 1948 (BELOW). Situated at the northern end of Washington Park (below), the 13-story, 225-room Park Lane was the brainchild of Philip Zang, who opened it in 1926. It was largely residential (rooms had kitchenettes); Broadway songwriter Vincent Youmans ("Tea for Two") occupied a suite during his frequent Denver stays. In 1948, Kansas City, Missouri, hotelier Benjamin F. Weinberg bought the hotel and opened the Top of the Park (above), a nightclub with dining, dancing, cocktails, and big-name entertainment. Comedian George Gobel first introduced his Lonesome George character here; other performers included Liberace, Dorothy Dandridge, Judy Canova, Tex Ritter, and Shecky Greene. Weinberg sought to operate it as a resort hotel, but its setting—neither country nor city—worked against it. The Park Lane was demolished in 1966. (Both, author's collection.)

SIXTEENTH STREET CHRISTMAS, 1937. Even during the Great Depression, Denver's main street, Sixteenth, got dressed up for the holidays. In this view looking northwest from Champa Street, the University Building, Joslins, and the Tabor Theater are visible at left, with S.H. Kress and May Company seen at right. The Daniels and Fisher Tower, complete with a lighted Santa Claus, crowns the scene. (HC, 10043991.)

DANIELS AND FISHER, c. 1958. William Bradley Daniels founded Denver's oldest department store in 1864, and William Garrett Fisher joined him in 1872. In 1875, they built a two-story block on the eastern corner of Sixteenth and Lawrence Streets, the genesis of this building. The tower (right), built in 1911 by son William Cooke Daniels remains, but the store closed in 1958 and was demolished in 1971. (DPL, X-22936.)

MAY COMPANY, C. 1925.
David May came to
Colorado in 1877, opening
a store in Leadville. He
transferred operations to
Denver in 1888, eventually
occupying a Lawrence
Street location across
from Daniels and Fisher.
In 1906, the firm, now a
growing chain, opened
this gleaming, white
terra-cotta-clad store on
the northern corner of
Sixteenth and Champa
Streets. A six-story
addition (right) was added
in 1925. (HC, 20007814.)

MAY-D&F INTERIOR, 1958. Both the Daniels and Fisher and May Company buildings closed when May-D&F, the result of their merger, opened at Sixteenth Street and Court Place in 1958. This 400,000-square-foot, five-level store with underground parking was the first major new downtown department store built in America after World War II. It closed in 1993 (see pages 116–117). (Bob Rhodes collection.)

J.C. PENNEY, 1935.
Across from the May Company, Frank Frewen and Earl Chester Morris designed this 1935 Art Moderne gem for the downtown J.C. Penney store, on the eastern corner of Sixteenth and Champa Streets. Penney built a larger building at Sixteenth and California Streets in 1952. That second store closed in 1981 and was demolished in 1982. This building still stands, but looks nothing like this. (Roger Whitacre collection.)

MODERNIZED STOREFRONTS, 1957. After Penney's moved, its building (right) was completely remodeled with windowless upper floors and rented to smaller stores, including Lerner Shops. In 1954, May Company (center) was similarly remodeled, just four years before relocating to Courthouse Square (page 116). Both projects were part of a wave of post–World War II modernizations that covered historical details with simpler, signage-dominated facades. (DPL, X-23049.)

DENVER DRY GOODS, c. 1965. Holiday finery illuminates the 400-foot-long aisle of the Denver Dry Goods, located at Sixteenth and California Streets. The successor to McNamara Dry Goods, it was named for its city after the earlier firm failed in 1893. Although the 350,000-square-foot building still stands, housing shops, offices, and residences, the store closed in 1987 following a merger with May Company. (HC, 10043981.)

GANO-DOWNS, c. 1959. Founded in 1882, the upscale clothing store Gano-Downs occupied the Steele Building (shown here after a 1952 modernization), on the eastern corner of Sixteenth and Stout Streets, for most of its history. In 1972, Hawaii-based Amfac bought Gano-Downs and moved its Joseph Magnin chain into the space. The building was demolished in 1980 for the Hudson's Bay Centre high-rise. (DPL, X-24025.)

NEUSTETER'S DOWNTOWN, 1924. Directly across Sixteenth Street from Gano-Downs, the upscale store founded by Max, Meyer, and Edward Neusteter in 1911 expanded in 1924 into a five-story building designed by William A. and Arthur E. Fisher. The first floor, shown here, included a series of Vance Kirkland murals depicting the history of fashion. The store closed in 1986; a drugstore occupies this space as of this writing. (HC, 10043983.)

NEUSTETER'S CHERRY CREEK, 1960. Neusteter's opened its Cherry Creek branch, at First Avenue and Milwaukee Street, in 1960. Designed by Paul Reddy, the store included a restaurant on the fourth floor. Financially strapped Neusteter's shuttered stores one by one in the 1980s, with Cherry Creek the last to close, in 1986. Later that year, Joyce Meskis moved her Tattered Cover Bookstore into the building, occupying it until 2006. (HC, 10027907.)

JOSLINS, C. 1990. An 1887 brick department store (now a hotel) hides under this 1965 modernization, a Richard L. Crowther design. John Jay Joslin founded his store in 1873, and the company operated here on the southern corner of Sixteenth and Curtis Streets until 1995, when it was the last downtown department store to close. The Joslin chain merged with Dillard's in 1998. (DPL, Z-10463.)

GOLDEN EAGLE, 1905. German immigrant Leopold Henry Guldman loved his adopted country and chose the name of the national bird to grace his Lawrence Street store, which opened in 1879. A master in writing advertising copy and offering low prices, Guldman was successful enough to expand his store to the western corner of Sixteenth and Lawrence Streets. The store closed in 1941, and the building was later demolished for urban renewal. (DPL, MCC-1871.)

Montgomery Ward, 1993. Built in 1929, the eight-story Montgomery Ward mail-order warehouse and retail store, on the west side of Broadway at Virginia Avenue, employed over 1,000 workers at its peak, spreading across 560,000 square feet. After Ward closed, a developer began renovating it for offices (as seen here) but lost project control in 1988. The building was imploded in 1993 for a shopping center. (Roger Whitacre collection.)

Downtown Woolworth's, c. 1970. Billed as the world's largest when it reached its full 173,000-square foot size, the F.W. Woolworth Company's downtown store opened in the Symes Building at Sixteenth and Champa Streets in the 1920s. It added the adjacent property (previously home to the *Denver Post*) in 1951 and in 1963 stretched the store to Fifteenth Street (right) with a two-story addition. The Woolworth's closed in 1994. (Rob Mohr collection.)

Three

URBAN REMOVAL

SKYLINE MODEL, 1967. Urban renewal, in the form of government-funded demolition of buildings considered dilapidated, was popular across America after World War II. Denver's 1967 Skyline plan, approved two-to-one by voters, called for demolishing 37 (later reduced to 27) downtown blocks and construction of a Skyline Freeway (foreground). The Denver Urban Renewal Authority (DURA) used this model to persuade voters; anticipated Skyline buildings are white. (DPL, WH2129RMN.)

LARIMER STREET, 1960 (ABOVE) AND 1971 (BELOW). A chief Skyline plan target was Larimer Street, immortalized by Jack Kerouac in *On the Road*, but considered an embarrassing, financially burdensome skid row by city business and government leaders. Pro-Skyline newspaper headlines emphasized easy availability of cheap liquor, with "One Tavern For Every 27 Residents." The 1500 block (above) was home to prominent early Denver businesses, most famously Fred Charpiot's restaurant, Delmonico's of the West. Clothier Joe Alpert (right) operated at the Fifteenth Street corner from 1910 until forced to relocate just outside the Skyline zone in 1973; other forced-out retailers, Dave Cook Sporting Goods and Robert Waxman Cameras, followed suit. The 1601 block (below) was once home to Richard Pinhorn's Manhattan Restaurant and the Arcade, Ed Chase's plush casino. (Above, DPL, Z-457; below, photograph by Thomas J. Noel.)

CITIZENS MISSION, 1953 (ABOVE) AND 1950 (BELOW). Rev. Ernest M. Baber directed Citizens Mission at 1617 Larimer Street (visible at left in the lower photograph on page 58) for 28 years. The minister, at left in both photographs on this page, advocated for the poor and maintained that city business interests actually preferred having a skid row, for easier recruitment of cheap day labor. Above, volunteers are helping unload locally grown produce in exchange for a free meal from the mission. Below, low-income downtown residents pass through a Christmas meal-serving line, in an annual dinner sponsored by the *Denver Post* and Mile-High Sertoma Club. Some of these people may have still been around in 1967, when a survey found approximately 1,800 residents living in the Skyline renewal area. (Both, HC, above, 10043997, below, 10043996.)

FUTURE LARIMER SQUARE, 1957. Initially intended for demolition when DURA began planning Skyline in the early 1960s, the 1400 block of Larimer Street was rescued when Dana Crawford formed Larimer Square Associates in 1963 and began renovating buildings to create Larimer Square. Some of the buildings in this photograph were on the DURA demolition list even after Crawford began, but she later was able to save them. (Thomas J. Noel collection.)

LARIMER STREET, C. 1895. The buildings just past Fifteenth Street on Larimer Street, seen in this image taken from what later became Larimer Square, would have been excellent candidates for renovation. The five-story Pioneer Building and the eight-story Railroad Building (left), along with the Good Block at the corner of Sixteenth Street, would have only grown in character and economic value had they been saved. (Author's collection.)

TABOR BLOCK, C. 1967. Once Denver's finest commercial edifice, "Silver King" Horace Tabor's 1879 building at Sixteenth and Larimer Streets was one of nine Skyline-area structures that the Denver Landmarks Commission proposed saving. DURA commissioner Alex Holland found it "hard to believe" that it possessed historical significance, sure that saving it would complicate the selling of adjacent land. Demolition came in 1972. (HC, 10043988, photograph by James O. Milmoe.)

CURTIS AND CLARKE BLOCK, C. 1967. Another lost landmark on the Landmarks Commission's list of buildings it called "familiar and dear to the people of Denver" and that should be preserved was the 1874 Curtis and Clarke Block at 1634 Larimer Street. Built by Denver Tramway Company cofounder Rodney Curtis, the building had housed state offices (including the governor's) from 1877 to 1880. (HC, 10043984, photograph by James O. Milmoe.)

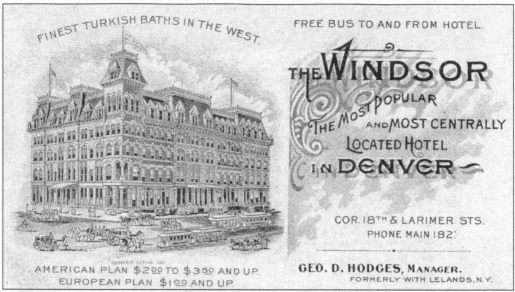

WINDSOR HOTEL, 1884. Denver's finest hotel upon its 1880 opening, the Windsor was built by James Duff, as agent for the British-funded Denver Mansions Company. Horace Tabor bought the lease and had his associate William Bush run it. The ballroom's floating dance floor was mounted on springs; the rooms boasted diamond-dust mirrors. The Windsor declined after Tabor died (in the hotel) in 1899, unable to compete with newer hotels. It was demolished in 1960, for parking. The Windsor is visible at Eighteenth and Larimer Streets (below, right). Across the street, closer to the photographer, the five-story Barclay Block (also on the Landmark Commission's preservation list) was built by the Denver Mansions Company in 1884; it served as the state capitol between 1885 and 1893. (Above, author's collection; below, DPL, photograph by R.M. Davis.)

MARKHAM HOTEL, C. 1895. One of Denver's oldest hostelries when it burned down in 1969, the Markham, originally with just three floors, opened in 1872 as Munger House, on the southern corner of Seventeenth and Lawrence Streets. In 1883, V.D. Markham, Thomas M. Patterson, and Charles S. Thomas bought it and remodeled it extensively. The ground floor was home to Patterson's *Rocky Mountain News* from 1897 to 1901. (DPL, H-559.)

GERMAN-AMERICAN TRUST COMPANY, 1910. Leading Denver German Americans, including Philip Zang, organized the German-American Trust Company in 1905, and commissioned Montana S. Fallis and John J. Stein to design its 1908 bank on the western corner of Seventeenth and Lawrence Streets. When the United States entered World War I in 1917, it became American Bank, and later, American National Bank. The building was demolished by DURA in 1971. (*DMF.*)

FEDERAL RESERVE BRANCH BANK, c. 1930. Faced in Colorado Yule marble, the Denver Branch of the Federal Reserve Bank of Kansas City opened in 1925 on the northern corner of Seventeenth and Arapahoe Streets. It moved to its current home on Sixteenth Street in 1968, and the old building was demolished in 1970. The Denver Public Library had proposed saving it, for a possible lower downtown branch. (HC, 20007762.)

IRON BUILDING, 1969. Also on the Landmark Commission's "should be preserved" list, the John W. Roberts–designed Iron Building, on the eastern corner of Seventeenth and Arapahoe Streets, opened in 1891 and came down in 1969. With cast-iron construction (the first such in Denver), it heralded the use of structural steel in the 20th century. A different two-story steel-and-glass structure occupies this corner today. (HC, 10043998.)

Seventeenth and Arapahoe Streets,
c. 1908. The John J. Huddart–designed
Bank Block dominates this view southwest
down Arapahoe Street. It shows Denver's
then intact urban fabric before the rise
of the automobile and the great visual
interest produced by relatively small
buildings grouped together. This was the
first block demolished for Skyline and the
first to be redeveloped, as Prudential (now
Independence) Plaza. (DPL, MCC-3739.)

Londoner Building, 1967. Grocer Wolfe
Londoner, who had been provisioning
Denverites since 1859, built this ornate
building (visible in the distance in the
previous photograph) for his store at
1624 Arapahoe Street in 1889. That
year, he was elected mayor, through
ballot-box stuffing (of which he claimed
ignorance); the scandal resulted in
his removal from office in 1891. The
basement housed the Cyclone Cellar, an
informal press club. (DPL, X-24878.)

CENTRAL BANK, 1911. Commanding the western corner of Fifteenth and Arapahoe Streets, Jules Jacques Benoit Benedict's masterful 1911 design for the Central Savings Bank (left) conveyed both grace, with its curved corner, and permanence. His sophisticated design carried through to the banking lobby (below), with its vaulted ceiling. The bank moved across Fifteenth Street in 1973 when Park Central (a Skyline project) was completed, but DURA kept its old home on its short list of buildings to be retained. Under a different owner, however, it eventually fell into foreclosure and ended up in the portfolio of a British bank that viewed it as a troubled asset. In 1989, that bank applied for a demolition permit, which the city could not legally deny. Mayor Federico Peña and DURA tried to intervene, and preservationists protested (page 2), but to no avail. (Both, *DMF.*)

CENTRAL BANK DRIVE-THROUGH, 1957. Bank president Elwood Brooks had a vision for the former Tramway Central Loop that surrounded Central Bank. Calling his new parking lot and drive-through facility Central Park was artful marketing, but the project was essentially suburban in both inspiration and execution. In 1962, Brooks and some associates formed Park City Realty to engage in private urban-renewal projects on nearby blocks. (DPL, C69-7.)

PEOPLE'S BANK, C. 1892. The nine-story, Frank E. Edbrooke–designed People's Bank rose on the southern corner of Sixteenth and Lawrence Streets in 1890. Demolition was imminent when its owners filed suit (ultimately losing) against DURA. They wanted to renovate and felt that DURA's offer of $200,000 was unfair. It was imploded on November 15, 1970, so that the Central Bank–anchored Park Central project could proceed. (HC, 20102520.)

MINING EXCHANGE, C. 1895 (LEFT) AND 1963 (BELOW). With its extensive ornamentation, miner statue–topped tower, and massive arched entry (flanked by busts of a bull and a bear, preserved today in Larimer Square), the exuberant 1891 Mining Exchange (left), by the St. Louis firm of H. William Kirchner and August Kirchner, dominated the southern corner of Fifteenth and Arapahoe Streets. When Central Bank president Elwood Brooks and some associates formed Park City Realty to engage in private urban renewal, its location directly opposite the bank made it an easy target. Below, Brooks (left) and Mayor Tom Currigan (right) watch the statue's removal; Central Bank is visible at left. The miner statue stands today in front of the Mining Exchange's replacement, the 42-story Brooks Towers residential building. (Both, HC, left, 20102540, below, 10043980.)

POST OFFICE AND CUSTOMS HOUSE,
C. 1895 (ABOVE) AND 1962 (RIGHT).
Another Park City Realty project
involved the block bounded by
Fifteenth, Sixteenth, Arapahoe, and
Curtis Streets. The General Services
Administration had declared the
Old Customs House (originally the
Denver Post Office) as surplus, and
Park City was the highest bidder in
a 1963 auction. After assembling
most of the other properties on the
block, including the Tabor Grand
Opera House (far left), Park City sold
the land to the Federal Reserve for
a new branch bank, replacing the
old one on Seventeenth Street. The
post office, authorized by Congress
in 1882 and completed in 1892, was
never adequate, and it was replaced
by a new building on Stout Street
in 1916. At right, the structurally
unsound cupola was removed a few
years before demolition. (Both, HC,
above, 20103656, right, 10043990.)

ERNEST AND CRANMER BUILDING, C. 1905.
Named for its builders, Finis P. Ernest and
William H.H. Cranmer, this Frank E.
Edbrooke–designed office block opened in
1891 on the southern corner of Seventeenth
and Curtis Streets. In a move similar to
Central Bank's private urban renewal,
neighboring Colorado National Bank
acquired all of the properties on its block and
demolished the Ernest and Cranmer in 1963
for drive-through banking. (DPL, MCC-327.)

QUINCY BUILDING, C. 1929. Built by Thomas M. Patterson and Charles S. Thomas in 1887, this
Frank E. Edbrooke–designed office block opposite Ernest and Cranmer was originally named for
its builders and then renamed Quincy 10 years later. It housed the *Rocky Mountain News* from 1887
to 1897, during the period when Patterson was acquiring control of the paper. The site became
a parking lot in the 1950s. (DPL, Rh-13.)

COOPER BUILDING, C. 1929 (ABOVE) AND 1970 (BELOW). Designed by Frank E. Edbrooke and erected in 1892, the eight-story Cooper Building (above) occupied the northern corner of Seventeenth and Curtis Streets. Diagonally opposite the Ernest and Cranmer Building, it was home to Denver National Bank between 1893 and 1928. With its corner drugstore and soda fountain, the building also served revelers enjoying the many entertainments of Curtis Street (see chapter 4); the Plaza (formerly the Crystal) and Rivoli (formerly the Paris) theaters are visible farther northeast along Curtis Street. It took DURA's demolition contractor eight seconds to implode it in 1970 (below). Note the Colorado National Bank drive-through facility visible at bottom, where the Ernest and Cranmer Building had stood. (Above, HC, 10044089; below, DPL, X-24929.)

CHAMBER OF COMMERCE BUILDING, C. 1915. On the northern corner of Fourteenth and Lawrence Streets, the 1885 Chamber of Commerce Building (yet another on the landmark commission's preservation wish list) was home to the Davis-Bridaham Drug Company at the time of this photograph. Considered one of Frank E. Edbrooke's minor masterpieces, the rusticated stone building later became a residential hotel and was demolished in 1967. (DPL, X-24200.)

SKYLINE PARK, 1974. The three-block Skyline Park, on Arapahoe Street from Fifteenth to Eighteenth Streets, was intended as the Skyline renewal district's centerpiece. Renowned landscape architect Lawrence Halprin won numerous awards for it. Poorly maintained and patronized by more homeless people than downtown interests were comfortable with (both conditions still true today), the Halprin design was radically altered in 2003 and was lost to future generations. (Photograph by Thomas J. Noel.)

CURRIGAN EXHIBITION HALL, 1969 (ABOVE) AND 2001 (BELOW). Stretching along Stout and Champa Streets southwestward from Fourteenth Street, Currigan Exhibition Hall counted as the city's financial contribution to the federally funded Skyline project (the US government required some financial commitment from the city before it would provide funds). Clad in locally produced Cor-Ten steel (designed to self-seal, rusting to a rich maroon shade), the 100,000-square-foot hall was column-free inside (below), thanks to its award-winning "space frame" design by William C. Muchow and a team of other local architects, and it was considered so futuristic when it opened that Woody Allen used it to film scenes for his science-fiction comedy *Sleeper* (1973). Expansion of the nearby Colorado Convention Center resulted in its 2002 demolition. (Above, Thomas J. Noel collection; below, Roger Whitacre collection.)

AURARIA, 1933 (ABOVE) AND C. 1972 (BELOW). After getting Skyline rolling, Denver Urban Renewal Authority next set its sights on another area deemed blighted. Auraria, the mixed neighborhood of houses, small businesses, and industries between Speer Boulevard, Colfax Avenue, and Wazee Street, was the oldest part of the city, founded in 1858. Home to successive waves of immigrants—German, Irish, Jewish, Hispanic—Auraria was one of several sites studied for locating Metropolitan State College, Community College of Denver, and the University of Colorado at Denver. Auraria was chosen for the campus in 1968, and DURA began buying properties, with demolition beginning in 1972. Don and Carolyn Etter, valuing Denver's oldest buildings, argued for preservation, and spearheaded the rescue of one block, today's Ninth Street Historic Park. The photograph above shows a 1933 flood. (Both, DPL, above, X-29314, below, WH1288.)

LINDELL HOTEL, 1940. Representative of Auraria's commercial buildings was the Lindell Hotel at Eleventh and Larimer Streets. Named for a St. Louis hostelry, the Lindell was originally a two-story structure built by pioneer merchant Frederick Z. Salomon. Leander McCarty, who worked for Salomon, added the third floor, tower, and name in 1878. By the time of its 1973 demolition, the structure had just two floors once again. (DPL, X-29808.)

ST. LEO'S CATHOLIC CHURCH, 1912. Auraria was once home to three Catholic congregations. German-founded St. Elizabeth's, at Eleventh and Curtis Streets, was consecrated in 1898. As Irish immigrants moved to Auraria, they needed their own church, and millionaire flour miller John Kernan Mullen helped fund St. Leo's, at Colfax Avenue and Tenth Street. It was demolished in 1965. St. James' Methodist Episcopal Church (also gone) is visible at left. (DMF.)

ST. CAJETAN SCHOOL, 1944. Mullen also helped fund St. Cajetan (built in 1926, now used for campus purposes), when Auraria's growing Hispanic population needed a church. St. Cajetan Parish built this 1936 grade school (demolished), designed by Temple Hoyne Buell, and ran a clinic, credit union, and convent. Auraria community members formed the Displaced Aurarians organization after they were forced to move. (DPL, X-28255.)

ST. ROSE RESIDENCE, C. 1967. Built by the Franciscan Sisters in 1890, the St. Rose (originally St. Rosa's) of Lima Residence for Women stood on the southern corner of Tenth and Champa Streets. This wing was added in 1918, and the entire structure was demolished in 1974 for construction of the Auraria Higher Education Center. (DPL, AUR000003, photograph by Don D. Etter.)

Four

AMUSEMENTS

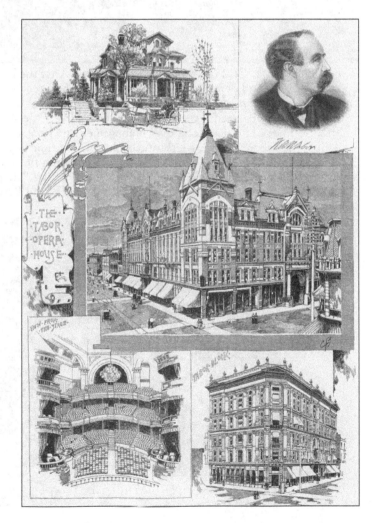

TABOR GRAND OPERA HOUSE, 1889. This illustration from *Frank Leslie's Illustrated Newspaper* shows the Tabor Grand Opera House (center and lower left), the Tabor Block (lower right), the second Tabor Mansion at Thirteenth Avenue and Sherman Street (upper left), and Horace Austin Warner Tabor himself. Colorado's then wealthiest man built the theater at Sixteenth and Curtis Streets in 1881, spending $750,000 on building and furnishings. (DPL, Z-8799.)

TABOR THEATER, C. 1912 (ABOVE) AND 1950 (BELOW). After the Panic of 1893, Horace Tabor lost control of the opera house, and by the early 1900s, it had become a vaudeville theater (above), ceding the higher-toned touring shows to the Broadway Theater uptown. In 1922, new owners remodeled it and renamed it the Colorado, offering live stage shows along with silent movies. Impresario Harry Huffman took over management in 1929, bringing back the Tabor name, launching the Taborettes chorus girls, and booking traveling acts such as the Andrews Sisters. Fox Intermountain Theaters later managed it, booking first-run films (below) and touring Broadway shows, but it soon became a B-movie house. Central Bank's Park City Realty demolished it in 1964 for development, but later sold the land to the Federal Reserve. (Above, DPL, Z-10314; below, author's collection.)

CURTIS STREET, 1913. The Tabor was grand, but it soon had rivals, with an entire entertainment district springing up around it. Between Fifteenth to Eighteenth Streets, Curtis Street by the 1910s was Denver's "Great White Way." City boosters compared it to New York's Broadway and boasted that Thomas Edison had proclaimed it "the best lighted street in the world." Theaters featuring movies and live acts were interspersed with cafés, bars, pool halls, candy shops, and other diversions. The 1920s represented the peak years for Curtis Street. By the end of that decade, with the construction of more elaborate movie palaces elsewhere, Curtis Street began to lose business. Some theaters went dark in the 1930s, but others held on until demolition for 1960s urban renewal. (Above, DPL, MCC-1901; below, Rob Mohr collection.)

RIALTO THEATER, 1922. Located at 1540 Curtis, the Rialto was built in 1912 as the United States Theater. Four years later, it was given the name Rialto. A 1,080-seat house, it was demolished in 1961, when its next-door neighbor, Joslins department store (visible at left), expanded. (DPL, X-24728.)

EMPRESS THEATRE, 1914. One of the last Curtis Street theaters to be demolished (in 1969, for the Skyline urban renewal project), the 1,400-seat Empress Theatre at 1621 Curtis Street opened in 1907 as the Majestic. The owners of the *Denver Post* owned the theater for many years. Oliver Hardy and Stan Laurel, George Burns and Gracie Allen, and Charlie Chaplin all played there. It was later renamed New Victory, showing adult films at the end. (*DMF.*)

AMERICA THEATER, 1926. Next to the Empress, and directly across Sixteenth Street from the Tabor, the America boasted the largest electrified sign on Curtis Street. Designed by William A. and Arthur E. Fisher, the America opened in 1916 and was operated by Universal Films. The Fishers commissioned Colorado artist Allen Tupper True to paint history-themed murals above both entrances (below). Denver audiences proved fickle, and the America struggled throughout most of its existence. Various promotions were held, including one (above) featuring city firemen. In another, stopped by the local humane society, 250 live turkeys were to be dropped from an airplane over the city. Harry Huffman took over in 1929 but operated it for only a short time. By 1933, it had been converted to Niesner's, a variety store. (Both, DPL, above, X-27579, below, X-24799.)

PRINCESS THEATER, 1911. Opposite the Empress, the 1,140-seat Princess Theater at 1620 Curtis Street opened in 1909. It was renamed the Victory in 1919, commemorating the Allied victory in World War I. Its neighbor across the alley, the May Company, demolished the theater in 1951 for an expansion of its department store, which was itself demolished in 1964. (DPL, MCC-1399.)

STRAND THEATER, 1921. In 1914, the Princess/Victory's near neighbor, the Strand, built by the Brown and Megahan Amusement Company at 1630 Curtis Street, opened on the site of an earlier theater named Isis (the first Isis). In 1925, it was remodeled and renamed the State Theater. It operated until 1952, when its cross-alley neighbor, Colorado National Bank, purchased the theater and demolished it for parking. (DPL, X-24735.)

PARIS THEATRE, 1913. Near Eighteenth Street at 1751 Curtis Street, the 2,100-seat Paris Theatre was built in 1913. Its attractions included both vaudeville and movies, with a cabaret in the basement. Renamed the Rivoli in 1917, it was the longtime venue for comedian Hoyt "Bozo" Smythe. The Rivoli closed in the mid-1930s and was demolished a decade later for parking. (DPL, MCC-1946.)

ISIS THEATER, 1914. Robert Roeschlaub designed one of the more ornate Curtis Street theaters, the Isis (the second Isis) at 1722 Curtis Street, for Sam Baxter in 1913. With 1,800 seats, the Isis featured Wurlitzer's first-ever four manual theater organ, which Baxter advertised as the world's largest. Fox Films later took over management, and the second Isis was demolished in 1954 for parking. (DPL, MCC-1945.)

CRYSTAL THEATRE, C. 1903. Opposite the Isis and abutting the Cooper Building (left), the 900-seat Crystal Theatre at 1721 Curtis Street opened in the 19th century as the Wonderland Bijou. It bore the Crystal name between 1903 and 1909, featuring vaudeville. Later, when it was known as the Plaza, it was primarily a movie theater. It was demolished in 1953 for parking. (DPL, MCC-4056.)

DENHAM THEATER, 1974. Built by New York theater producers Jacob and Lee Shubert in 1913 as a legitimate theater, the Denham did not become a cinema until 1930. Architect Frank McClure designed a neoclassical six-story office building atop the theater, which was located on the eastern corner of Eighteenth and California Streets. It was demolished in 1974, for a parking garage. (Photograph by Thomas J. Noel.)

ORPHEUM THEATER, 1929 (ABOVE) AND 1950 (BELOW). Morris Meyerfield and Martin Beck, who in 1899 had founded the Orpheum Circuit of vaudeville theaters, built Denver's 1,600-seat Orpheum Theater, at 1537 Welton Street, in 1903 (above). With Meyerfield and Beck dominating vaudeville bookings in the western United States, Denver's Orpheum featured such names as Sophie Tucker, Will Rogers, the young Marx Brothers, and Bert Williams. After Orpheum merged with two other concerns, forming Radio-Keith-Orpheum (RKO) in 1928, the new company demolished the theater and built a new Orpheum in its place, opening it in 1932 (below). This new movie palace operated until 1967, when it was demolished for parking. In its last years, it was the RKO International 70, home to Denver's first 70-millimeter projector. (Both, DPL, above, X-24697, below, X-24688.)

BROADWAY THEATER, 1915 (ABOVE) AND 1921 (BELOW). Stage and screen legend Al Jolson (seated at center and wearing a light suit, below) was just one of many big-name actors to perform at the Broadway Theater. A Moorish fantasy featuring a scalloped proscenium and onion dome–topped boxes, it instantly became Denver's most prestigious theater, eclipsing the Tabor Grand, when it opened at 1756 Broadway in 1890. The theater could seat 1,620 audience members, who entered the lobby through a massive arch on Broadway. Actors used the stage door on Lincoln Street. (Above, HC, 20103548; below, DPL, Z-1149.)

HOTEL METROPOLE, C. 1900 (ABOVE) AND BROADWAY THEATER DEMOLITION, 1955 (RIGHT). Located directly across Broadway from the Brown Palace Hotel (the shadow of which is visible at bottom right, above), the Broadway Theater was attached to the Hotel Metropole. Owner William H. Bush commissioned architect Frank E. Edbrooke, who had also designed the Brown, to create both. The hotel operated Broadway Gardens (left, above) for its guests; the Cosmopolitan Hotel would later be built on the site and the Metropole incorporated into it. The Broadway was converted to show movies, and during the Great Depression it came under the management of Harry Huffman. The theater was demolished (right) in 1955 for a proposed hotel expansion that was never built. The site remained a parking lot for six decades. (Both, DPL, above, MCC-380, right, X-24818.)

DENVER THEATER, 1947 (ABOVE) AND 1980 (BELOW). Inspired by French Renaissance architecture, designed by William Norman Bowman, and constructed at a cost of $2 million, the city's namesake theater opened in 1927, just in time for the advent of talkies (although the first booking, *She's a Sheik*, was silent). The lobby, which fronted Sixteenth Street (above, right), was 100 feet long, with a side entrance on Glenarm Place (left); it wrapped around the two-story Powers-Behen menswear shop, a space later occupied by Walgreen Drugs and still later by Skaggs Drugs. The ornate Sixteenth Street facade was modernized in 1954 and the theater converted to a twin cinema in 1972. The Denver was demolished in 1980 for a proposed 57-story office tower that was never built; the Denver Pavilions retail/entertainment complex occupies the site today. (Above, HC, 10038452; below, DPL; X-24603.)

ALADDIN THEATRE, 1981 (ABOVE) AND 1927 (RIGHT). Harry Huffman built the Taj Mahal–inspired Aladdin Theatre at 2010 East Colfax Avenue (above) in 1926. Although an Indian landmark inspired the architecture, Huffman chose the Arabian name Aladdin because he wanted it to appear under A in the telephone book. Architect Frederick W. Ireland Jr. utilized a variety of theatrical effects to create a sense of wonder, including 2,500 fairy lights in the ceiling simulating the night sky and a projector that added clouds to the scene. After passing through the fanciful polychrome terra-cotta entrance (right), patrons could pause to enjoy fountains and exotic plants before passing into the auditorium. It was demolished, with little warning, in 1984; a drugstore occupies the site today. (Above, Roger Whitacre collection; right, DPL, X-24787.)

MISSION THEATER, 1929.
The Mission Theater, opened in 1910 at 1465 South Pearl Street, is an example of the many small theaters that once dotted Denver's neighborhoods. Most of these small cinemas were located in business districts that grew up around streetcar lines. The Mission later became the Vogue, showing art films. It was converted to condominiums in 2001. (DPL, X-24684.)

WEBBER THEATER, 1948. One of the most attractive neighborhood theaters was built by attorney-turned-showman DeWitt C. Webber at 119 South Broadway in 1917. Webber, who lived in an upstairs apartment, had helped to incorporate the Town of South Denver and been partners in the Iris and Isis Theaters on Curtis Street. The Webber still stands, but it has been remodeled so as to be unrecognizable. (DPL, Z-10221.)

BAUR'S CURTIS STREET, 1943 (ABOVE) AND UPTOWN, 1947 (BELOW). Before or after a show, the original Baur's confectionery and tea room at 1512 Curtis Street (above) was the place to go. Otto Paul Baur, having founded the firm in 1872, claimed in a 1902 interview to have invented the ice-cream soda; his assertion has never been decisively proven—nor disproven. Baur's occupied the Curtis Street building continuously from 1891 until 1970, when a later owner converted it to a seafood restaurant; the building still stands. Baur's Uptown (below) opened in the Empire Building on the southern corner of Sixteenth Street and Glenarm Place in 1938, serving shoppers and patrons of the nearby Denver, Orpheum, and Paramount Theaters. It closed in 1968, and the site is now occupied by the Denver Pavilions. (Above, DPL, X-29500; below, HC, 10038956.)

DUTCH MILL, 1915. Sheet-music publisher Theron C. Bennett opened the Dutch Mill in the Odd Fellows Hall at 1545 Champa Street in 1915. Popular with theatergoers, as well as with actors and musicians, it featured a small orchestra on the mezzanine, along with a lighted windmill with arms that turned slowly. Wait staff wore Dutch costumes, including wooden shoes. It closed in 1935. (DPL, X-29487.)

APPLE TREE SHANTY, C. 1965. Other Dutch-themed restaurants operated after the Dutch Mill closed. In 1948, the Apple Tree Shanty opened at 8710 East Colfax Avenue, remaining popular for decades. Staffed by Apple Tree Girls, who curtsied at the end of the meal, the menu featured barbecue, with hot apple muffins on the side. The restaurant closed after moving to the Denver Tech Center in the late 1970s. (Author's collection.)

NORMANDY FRENCH RESTAURANT, C. 1965. Opened at 4900 East Colfax Avenue by Frenchman Lucien Broch in 1952, the Normandy's rustic decor evoked a French country inn. In 1958, Heinz Gerstle and his cousin Pierre Wolfe bought it, continuing to serve French *cuisine du marché* ("fresh cuisine of the marketplace"). It moved to 1515 Madison Street in 1972, and the building was converted to another French eatery, Tante Louise. (Author's collection.)

THE QUORUM, C. 1965. After partnering on the Normandy, in 1960 Pierre Wolfe opened his own fine-dining establishment, the Quorum, in the Argonaut Hotel at Colfax Avenue and Grant Street. Wolfe, also a radio and television personality, won *Holiday* magazine's Distinctive Dining award several years running and once turned away Marlon Brando for not wearing a jacket. Wolfe, saddening Denver's old guard, closed the restaurant in 1990. (Author's collection.)

NORTH WOODS INN, C. 1969. In 1942, King and Evelyn Hudson opened the Country Kitchen at 6115 South Santa Fe Drive in Littleton. Two decades later, their log cabin restaurant, leased by Raymond Dambach, reopened as the popular North Woods Inn, complete with a giant statue of Paul Bunyan outside. New customers immediately noticed the peanut shells that crunched underfoot, purposely thrown on the floor by diners; the restaurant served 1,200 pounds of unshelled peanuts per month. All drinks, even wine, were served in large steins, the huge, multicourse meals were difficult to finish, and the seasoning used on the tasty cottage cheese inspired many home cooks to try replicating it. A new owner moved the operation to Douglas County in 1997, where it closed in 2011. The log cabin remains, as part of Hudson Gardens. (Both, author's collection.)

JOE "AWFUL" COFFEE, C. 1955. Russian immigrant Joseph Rutkofsky had been a regional featherweight boxing champion when he opened his Ringside Lounge (above) on Seventeenth Street, near Arapahoe Street, in 1943. His name derived from an early bout when the announcer could not pronounce his name, and a Denver sportswriter made up a new one on the spot. A generous man, Coffee donated to many charities; below, he hosts a birthday party for orphaned children. According to a newspaper account, "No person was ever turned away from Coffee's whether he had money to pay for the meal or not." The restaurant stayed open until midnight and was decorated with autographed photographs of boxing greats, along with caricatures by famous cartoonists. Coffee closed the Ringside Lounge in 1965 and died in 1994. (Above, Rob Mohr collection; below, DPL, X-19548.)

WHITE SPOT, 1947 (LEFT) AND C. 1960 (BELOW). With just a $1,500 investment, William F. Clements opened the first White Spot at 22 South Broadway in 1947 (left). By the time of his 1969 death, after which his widow, Ruby, and son Tony led the firm, he had built it into a chain of nine Denver-area coffee shops, including one at 2000 South Broadway (below). Some were owned by their managers, including Spero Armatas, whose descendants later turned the downtown White Spot into the popular restaurant Sam's No. 3. William's brother George Clements had a similar operation, Georgy's, at Speer and Federal Boulevards. William also opened a restaurant at Alameda Avenue and Sheridan Boulevard known as the Colonel, featuring the fried-chicken recipe of that well-known Kentuckian Col. Harlan Sanders. (Both, HC, left, 10043982, below, 10044088.)

THE LAST WHITE SPOT, 2001. Many of the White Spots were designed by Louis Armét and Eldon C. Davis of Los Angeles, who worked in the Googie style popularized in Southern California. With its W roofline, the last remaining White Spot, shown here at 800 Broadway, closed in 2001 and was demolished, although a few White Spot buildings remain around the city, operating under other names. (Roger Whitacre collection.)

DENVER DRUMSTICK, C. 1964. Another chain built in Googie style, Denver Drumstick opened its first location on West Colfax Avenue, designed by Denver's W. Dan Rohwer, in 1955. Austin Myers, a Texas poultry rancher, started the chain, which he built up to nine locations, as a way of creating demand for his chickens. The original Drumstick featured a 600-foot-long miniature railroad to entertain the children. (Author's collection.)

HAMBURGERS BY ROCKYBILT, 1980. A secret sauce made of mustard, relish, Heinz 57, and catsup drew diners to Rockybilt, where they were asked "With or without?" (onions) and from which they could "tak-homa-sak" of burgers. Roy Chesney opened the first of 12 Rockybilts in 1936 on East Colfax Avenue. This last one, on the southeast corner of Speer and Federal Boulevards, closed in 1980. (Roger Whitacre collection.)

SCOTCHMAN MENU, C. 1965. Opened by Herman Christoffers in 1949, and taken over by his nephew Carl Cerveny in 1953, the Scotchman, at 4960 Federal Boulevard, was one of Denver's most popular drive-in restaurants, especially after a cruise down Sixteenth Street, until its 1977 closure. "Our food is horrible, so is the service," joked the restaurant, its menu featuring "Choking Cokes," "Horrible Burgers," and "Exquisite Messes." (Dave Metcalfe collection.)

LEO'S PLACE, 1973. In 1970, Leo Goto, Howard Torgrove, and Larry Atler opened the popular Leo's Place on the southeast corner of Sixteenth Avenue and Broadway, furnishing it with crystal chandeliers from Baur's, lighting from the Federal Reserve Bank, lions from the Shirley-Savoy Hotel, and other pieces of Denver's past. The Regional Transportation District demolished it in 1980, for Civic Center Station. (Photograph by Thomas J. Noel.)

MUDDY WATERS OF THE PLATTE, 1977. Joe DeRose founded Muddy's at 2557 Fifteenth Street in 1975. Open until 4:00 am daily, the coffee house served as a kind of community center for Denver's underground art scene, with a used bookstore, vintage clothing store, and the Slightly Off Center Theatre subletting space. A new building owner evicted Muddy's and the other concerns in 1985. (Photograph by Thomas J. Noel.)

CASTLE OF CULTURE AND COMMERCE, 1949. John Brisben Walker, an entrepreneur with wide interests (including *Cosmopolitan* magazine) opened River Front Park on the eastern bank of the South Platte River between Sixteenth and Nineteenth Streets in 1887. The park included a race track, ballpark, skating rink, canoeing, and boating, but its centerpiece was this castle, as seen from the Sixteenth Street viaduct. As the Castle of Culture and Commerce, it originally housed art, mineral, and agricultural exhibits, until Walker sold the park in 1891. The Walker Castle, as it was known, was later used by the Denver and Salt Lake Railway (the Moffat Road) for storage. Its remains were demolished after a spectacular fire leveled it in 1951. The River Front Park site was eventually given over to various railroad and industrial uses but was redeveloped by the city in 2001 into Commons Park. The castle stood approximately where the park's man-made hill rises today. (DPL, X-24964.)

LUNA PARK, C. 1910. Sloan's Lake reflects the lights of this amusement park, which once stood at the lake's northwestern corner. Opened as Sloan's Lake Resort in 1890, renamed Manhattan Beach in 1891, and then Luna Park in 1909, the park experienced devastating fires and financial difficulties throughout its history, permanently closing in 1914, unable to compete with nearby Lakeside and Elitch Gardens. (Rob Mohr collection.)

ELITCH'S MAIN GATE, 1934. John and Mary Elitch founded Elitch Gardens in 1890, in what had been the Chilcott Farm at West Thirty-eighth Avenue and Tennyson Street (today's street names). By the time of this Depression-era photograph, Arnold Gurtler owned the amusement park. The park's location on multiple streetcar lines made it a popular summer destination for people living in all parts of Denver. (HC, 10027956.)

WORLD-FAMOUS ELITCH GARDENS, 1993. A 1958 street-widening project necessitated removal of the main gate (previous page) and its replacement by this parabolic arch designed by architect Paul R. Reddy. Supported by two 71-foot-tall pylons, the steel arch was covered by white fiberglass, backlit at night by neon. The arch is demolished, but the low planters in front remain on the corner today. (Roger Whitacre collection.)

TROCADERO BALLROOM, C. 1970. John Mulvihill bought Elitch's in 1916, after Mary Elitch experienced financial difficulties. Mulvihill's first big change was to build the Trocadero Ballroom, opened in 1917. During the big-band era, many of the biggest acts played the "Troc," including the Dorsey Brothers, Benny Goodman, Les Brown, Gene Krupa, Guy Lombardo, and Harry James. Elitch's demolished the ballroom in 1975, to general sadness. (Suzanne Ryan collection.)

ELITCH THEATRE PROGRAM, 1974. Mary Elitch built Elitch Theatre in the park in 1891 as a memorial to her late husband. Initially, it was a vaudeville house, but in 1897, she instituted what would become America's oldest summer theater, with hundreds of plays produced over the decades. While the Elitch Theatre still stands, the traditional summer play season ended in 1991. (Author's collection.)

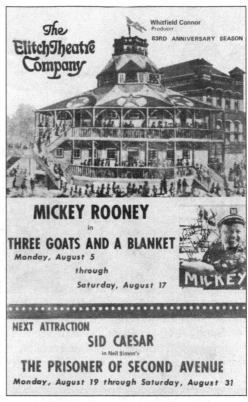

ACTOR'S PICNIC, 1965. Big-name actors regularly graced the stages of Elitch's and Central City Opera, which used to produce plays alongside opera. Here, members of both companies mingle at Elitch Gardens. Pictured are, from left to right, (first row) Monica Moran, Tom Helmore, Kitty Carlisle, Patricia Cutts, and Richard Roat; (second row) Whitfield Connor, George Gaynes, Brad Hatton, and Lawrence Weber. Connor and Hatton were Elitch Theatre producers. (David Forsyth collection.)

SANDY AND BUDD GURTLER, 1987. After World War II, Arnold Gurtler (John Mulvihill's son-in-law) brought his sons Jack and Budd into park management. In 1985, Budd (right) made his son Sandy (left) president. Budd had transformed Elitch's into a more thrill ride–oriented park, finding inventive ways to squeeze evermore rides (including the Turn of the Century, right) into the park's small footprint. (David Forsyth collection.)

VIEW FROM THE WILDCAT, C. 1975. The Wildcat, built in 1922, was not Elitch's first roller coaster (that had been the 1904 Toboggan 8), but it was the longest-lived. In this view, its safety rail is visible at lower left, while other portions weave through the Mister Twister; the section of roller coaster visible beyond the far clump of trees belongs to the Wildcat. (David Forsyth collection.)

MISTER TWISTER, C. 1975. Here are two views of one of the great lost roller coasters of America, Mister Twister (the relocated Elitch Gardens has a similar ride, Twister II). At right, riders experience the coaster's double loop; the miniature train ride's station is in the lower right. Below, people wait on the platform, with a previous group of riders just coming into the station in the distance. Built by the Philadelphia Toboggan Company and opened in 1965, Mister Twister featured an 80-foot drop and a pitch-black tunnel. When Sandy Gurtler became president, he looked to move the park to larger quarters. After Highlands Ranch residents objected to the Gurtlers' plan to relocate to that suburb, Elitch Gardens instead chose a site on the South Platte River near downtown. The old park's last year of operation was 1994. (Both, David Forsyth collection.)

ABANDONED ELITCH'S, 1995. After the downtown move, the old Elitch site was redeveloped into Highlands' Garden Village, with residential and retail components. Before demolition for that project, photographer Roger Whitacre was allowed access to the site on a crisp winter's day. At left, the high point of the Wildcat overlooks the Splinter log flume ride's splashdown pool, which threaded its way around and through the Wildcat—as seen by the gap (right) in the coaster's structure, through which the Splinter ran. Below, the Splinter's concrete chute wraps around the Wildcat's first turn, leading to the first hill; the Tennyson Street fence encloses Elitch's on the right. On the left, the two rides' boarding areas were largely destroyed in a 1995 arson incident. (Both, Roger Whitacre collection.)

BROADWAY PARK, 1910. With home plate located near Sixth Avenue and Bannock Street, Broadway Park was built by George Tebeau, "the father of Colorado baseball," in 1893, and was home to the minor-league Denver Bears baseball team after 1900. Although conveniently located, its grandstands shaded only some of its spectators, and the outfield had to be reconfigured when Speer Boulevard was built. (*DMF.*)

MERCHANTS PARK, C. 1922. The Denver Bears moved to Merchants Park in 1922, when funds provided by the Merchants Biscuit Company allowed the 1901 Union Park at Broadway and Virginia Avenue to be enlarged. Home to the Denver Post Tournament for its entire history, Merchants Park saw exhibition play by such greats as Babe Ruth, Lou Gehrig, and Satchel Paige. Installation of lights in the 1930s allowed nighttime play. (DPL, Rh-1330.)

MILE HIGH STADIUM, C. 1968. Bears Stadium, built into a hillside at Twentieth Avenue and Clay Street, replaced Merchants Park in 1948. The Denver Broncos began playing at Bears Stadium in 1960, and the facility was renamed Mile High Stadium in 1968 after a major expansion added additional decks to the original structure. It was demolished in 2002, after a new stadium opened nearby. (Thomas J. Noel collection.)

UNIVERSITY OF DENVER HILLTOP STADIUM, C. 1948. Built in 1925 for the DU Pioneers football team, Hilltop Stadium (upper right) served the university until the sport became too expensive for the school to support. Football play ended in 1961, and the stadium came down a decade later. Opposite the stands, the cavernous field house, a World War II–surplus donation by the federal government, stood until 1997. (Author's collection.)

McNichols Arena, c. 1990. Officially named for then mayor William H. McNichols Jr.'s father, and built for the voter-rejected 1976 Denver Winter Olympics, McNichols Arena ("Big Mac") opened in 1975 near Colfax Avenue and Federal Boulevard as the home of the Denver Rockets (later Nuggets) basketball team. The arena was demolished for the new Mile High Stadium after the privately financed Pepsi Center opened in 1999. (HC, 10043999.)

Denver Symphony Program, 1964. Isaac Stern was the featured soloist for this Denver Symphony Orchestra concert given at the Auditorium Theater (now the Ellie Caulkins Opera House). Denver had had orchestras since the 1880s, but the Denver Symphony was not founded until 1934, when it was organized as a fully professional orchestra, evolving from the semiprofessional Denver Civic Symphony, which had been founded in 1922. (Suzanne Ryan collection.)

Thirtieth Season   Fourteenth Concert

DENVER SYMPHONY ORCHESTRA

SAUL CASTON
Music Director and Conductor

TUESDAY EVENING, FEBRUARY 25, 1964—8:30 p.m.

Auditorium Theater

Soloist—ISAAC STERN, Violinist

Program

OVERTURE TO "THE BARTERED BRIDE"................................*Smetana*

CONCERTO FOR VIOLIN AND ORCHESTRA,
NO. 1 IN G MINOR ....*Bruch*

    I.   Allegro moderato
   II. Adagio
  III. Allegro energico

             Mr. Stern

Intermission

"POEME" FOR VIOLIN AND ORCHESTRA, OPUS 25 ....*Chausson*
             Mr. Stern

"CAPRICCIO ITALIEN," OPUS 45............................*Tschaikowsky*

Patrons are not admitted during the playing of a composition for the obvious reason that their entrance will disturb their neighbors. For the same reason considerate persons will not leave during the playing.

Concert starts promptly at 8:30 o'clock

Programs subject to unavoidable change

— 5 —

109

DENVER SYMPHONY ORCHESTRA · 1951-52 SEASON
Saul Caston, Musical Director and Conductor

DENVER SYMPHONY ORCHESTRA, 1951 (ABOVE) AND CHARLIE BURRELL, C. 1977 (LEFT). Horace Tureman was the founding conductor of the Denver Symphony, turning over his baton to Saul Caston in 1945. Maestro Caston conducted the increasingly popular and well-regarded orchestra for nearly two decades before resigning in 1964. After a period of turmoil, conductor Brian Priestman rescued the ailing ensemble in 1969, leading it to new artistic heights and popularity, with summer concerts in city parks, until resigning in 1977. Saul Caston had helped break the racial barrier in American orchestras by hiring bass viol player Charles "Charlie" Burrell, sometimes called the "Jackie Robinson of classical music," in 1949. Burrell, who also played jazz, later joined the San Francisco Symphony Orchestra, returning to Denver in 1965, where he played until retirement in 1999. (Both, Colorado Symphony Orchestra collection.)

DENVER SYMPHONY MARATHON, C. 1978. KVOD radio program director John Wolfe initiated the first Denver Symphony Marathon, held in February 1974. Over the following decade, the annual fundraiser, organized by Suzanne Ryan and hosted by the downtown May-D&F store, elicited participation by a wide cross-section of Denverites (maestro Brian Priestman called it "a symbol for a better life in Denver"). Over 66 hours, donors could request particular music be played, or purchase donated premiums, including items sold under a colorful tent, designed by architect Peter Dominick, hanging on the side of the store's hyperbolic paraboloid (above). Musicians also performed live in the store's windows; below, flautists Maralyn Prestia (left) and Pamela Endsley (center) chat with Wolfe. The Denver Symphony gave its final performance in 1989, reorganizing as the Colorado Symphony Orchestra in 1990. (Both, Suzanne Ryan collection.)

WAX MUSEUM, C. 1972. Meant to educate and entertain, the Wax Museum, at 919 Bannock Street, opened in 1964. The nearly 100 wax figures of historical subjects were actually made of vinyl, with glass eyes and human hair. J. Alfred Ritter led the museum, which closed in the early 1980s. The Forney Museum of Transportation later bought the figures, some of which can be seen there today. (Author's collection.)

MOUNT EVANS CREST HOUSE, C. 1950. Built in 1941 at the summit of Mount Evans (elevation 14,271 feet) by William Thayer Tutt of Colorado Springs and James Quigg Newton Jr. of Denver, the Crest House served coffee and doughnuts to generations of tourists and Denverites. Edwin Francis designed the unique rock structure to harmonize with the mountain. A botched propane delivery caused an explosion and fire in 1979. (Author's collection.)

Five

JUST YESTERDAY

JUDICIAL/HERITAGE CENTER, C. 1977. Completed in 1977 to a design by Rogers Nagel Langhart Architects, the Judicial/Heritage Center housed the Colorado State Museum in a gray-brick wedge-shaped building (center) and the Colorado Supreme Court in a granite-clad five-story tower (left). Nicknamed "the typewriter and the toaster" for their shapes, they were demolished in 2010 for the Ralph L. Carr Justice Center. (Photograph by Thomas J. Noel).

BOETTCHER ELEMENTARY SCHOOL, 1991 (ABOVE) AND 1940 (BELOW). Considered revolutionary when completed in 1940, this public school for children with disabilities was largely paid for by "cement king" Charles Boettcher. Architect Burnham Hoyt, working in the International Style, designed a series of ramps to allow wheelchair-bound students to move between levels without relying on help. It was located near Children's Hospital, at Nineteenth Avenue and Downing Street, and connected to that institution via underground tunnel. The Denver Public Schools closed the facility in the 1980s after determining the children's needs were best met by placing them in regular schools. After selling the building to the hospital, the latter institution (since relocated) demolished it in 1992 for parking, despite pleas from preservationists and former students to give the former school landmark status. (Above, Roger Whitacre collection; below, DPL, Z-10052.)

MILE HIGH CENTER, 1959. Although the tower at Seventeenth Avenue and Broadway (on the right in the image at right) remains standing, the original essence of architect I.M. Pei's design has been lost. Built by William Zeckendorf in 1956, Mile High Center was defined by a sense of order and optimism. The tower, with its plaid curtain wall of black, gray, and beige panels, stood in an intimate plaza, complete with waterfall, fountains, and reflecting pool, flanked by a low-rise banking hall and a hyperbolic-arched pavilion. Below, this view of the pavilion's elegant Matchless restaurant looks across the pool toward the tower's base. The composition was ruined in 1980, when the complex was integrated with the Philip Johnson–designed One United Bank Center across Lincoln Street. The pavilion was demolished and the plaza enclosed within a glass atrium that also obscures much of the tower. (Both, author's collection.)

COURTHOUSE SQUARE, C. 1965. Another Zeckendorf-Pei collaboration, Courthouse Square was so named because it stood on the site of the original county courthouse (page 28). The city sold the land to Zeckendorf's New York–based Webb and Knapp development company after World War II. He promised Denver a "second Radio City," akin to New York's Rockefeller Center, and delivered a two-block complex flanking Court Place along Sixteenth Street, anchored by the May-D&F department store and Denver Hilton Hotel (above). Pei designed a concrete glass-walled hyperbolic paraboloid as May-D&F's entrance and placed a sunken plaza (later named for Zeckendorf), used for ice-skating in winter and various events during warmer weather, between the paraboloid and the hotel (below). Pei designed the four elements—hotel, store, paraboloid, plaza—as a group, a composition that is now lost. (Above, author's collection; below, Rob Mohr collection.)

HYPERBOLIC PARABOLOID, 1988. After the Republic Building (page 44) was replaced by the towering 56-story Republic Plaza (left), and the Majestic (page 44), Metropolitan and other buildings gave way to twin, mirror-glass office buildings (center); the hyperbolic paraboloid's graceful design harmonized this array of high-rise towers. The downtown May-D&F closed in 1993, and a St. Louis–based hotelier eventually gained control of the Courthouse Square complex, intending to convert the vacant store into additional hotel rooms. The city, which had a new convention center but no 1,000-room headquarters hotel for large conventions, was eager to cooperate when the hotelier proposed demolishing the paraboloid, building an elegant box in its place, and adding several floors to the former department store. Preservationists, championing adaptive reuse of the paraboloid, fought the idea. The Denver Landmarks Commission designated it a landmark, but city council, along with the Denver Urban Renewal Authority and Downtown Denver, Inc., took the hotelier's side, awarding him a $33-million subsidy. The paraboloid's 1996 demolition still dismays those who loved the iconic structure. (Roger Whitacre collection.)

CENTRE THEATER, 1980 (LEFT) AND 1954 (BELOW). A crowd of 5,000 fans turned out during a late April snowstorm to greet Hollywood stars flown in for the grand opening of the first post–World War II downtown movie theater built in the United States (below). Located on Sixteenth Street between Cleveland Place and Court Place, the 1,247-seat Centre featured a steeply raked auditorium and curved 60-foot-wide screen. At the opening, Ethel Merman sang "There's No Business Like Show Business," followed by short speeches given by Bud Abbott and Lou Costello, Rita Moreno, Mary Pickford, and other luminaries. Architect Walter H. Simon and Denver's Art Neon Company created a memorably baroque 100-foot-tall marquee that could be seen for blocks. The Centre was demolished in 1981 for an office building. (Both, DPL.)

Century 21 Theater, 1979 (above) and 1966 (below). Located on South Colorado Boulevard between Arizona and Arkansas Avenues, the 1,048-seat Century 21 opened in 1966, as part of the final wave of single-screen first-run movie theaters to open in Denver. For ideal acoustics, Denver architect Richard L. Crowther designed a building with no right angles. The structure was dramatic inside and out, with a wedge-shaped copper-clad roof that cantilevered over the driveway to form a porte cochere, and circular, semi-recessed "celestial" light fixtures in the lobby ceiling. The concession stand was 39 feet long, and the screen, for 70-millimeter projection, was 60 feet wide and 26 feet high. After decades showing first-run hits, the Century 21 closed in 1993, and the building was demolished in 2012. (Both, DPL.)

COOPER THEATER, C. 1961 (ABOVE) AND 1980 (LEFT). Even more impressive than the Century 21 was the Cooper, on Colorado Boulevard at Tennessee Avenue (above). The Joseph H. Cooper Foundation hired Richard L. Crowther to create the 814-seat Cooper, opened in 1961, as the first theater designed especially for the three-projector "Cinerama" experience. Its 146-degree-arc screen, at 105 feet wide by 36 feet high, was thought to be the world's largest. The curving-walled, steeply raked auditorium immersed the audience. The exterior, a dramatic drum-shaped building, was painted a vivid bittersweet burnt orange. Bookings were mostly exclusive during the first weeks of a run. Memorable to those of a certain age, each of the three original *Star Wars* episodes (left) played for months to sold-out houses. The Cooper was demolished in 1994 for a bookstore. (Above, author's collection; left, DPL.)

CELEBRITY SPORTS CENTER, C. 1974 (ABOVE) AND 1961 (RIGHT). A block north of the Cooper Theater, on Colorado Boulevard at Kentucky Avenue, Celebrity Sports Center (above) provided joy to millions for 33 years. Conceived of by a Hollywood attorney with famous clients, Celebrity Bowling, Inc. was formed in 1959 by several well-known names, and a search began for a suitable site. Denver was chosen due to its rapid growth but possibly also because one of the investors, Walt Disney, just liked Colorado. Other famous names in the group included Jack Benny (right, flanked by Celebrity's general manager Richard Fletcher and an unidentified woman), John Payne, Bing Crosby, Art Linkletter, Spike Jones, Charles Laughton, Burl Ives, George Burns, Gracie Allen, Fibber McGee and Molly, and Disney's brother Roy O. Disney and nephew Roy E. Disney. (Both, David Forsyth collection.)

CELEBRITY SWIMMING POOL, 1961 (ABOVE) AND 1966 (BELOW). The complex opened in stages, with the Olympic-size (164 feet, one inch) swimming pool, with nine lanes and five diving boards (below) debuting in 1961. Designed to host competitions, it had risers for spectators. At its grand opening (above), Jimmie Dodd, emcee of the *Mickey Mouse Club* (at microphone), Mickey Mouse (left), and some Old West gunmen entertain the crowd. With other celebrities disappointed by the profits, Disney bought out the group in 1962. With Celebrity, Disney hoped to create a place where idle youths could stay out of trouble. He died in 1966, but Walt Disney Productions continued to operate it until 1979, when the company sold it to a group that included local businessmen. The new owners added three popular waterslides to the pool. (Both, David Forsyth collection.)

BOWLING TEAM, C. 1962 AND BOWLING LANES, 1994. Everything about Celebrity's bowling operation, which opened in 1960, before the rest of the complex, was superlative. It took 35 semitrailers to deliver the $1.25 million order for bowling equipment, purportedly "the largest single order for such equipment in U.S. history," according to newspaper accounts. The 80 lanes were built with 58 miles of lumber, 2.5 tons of nails, 15,000 screws, and 350 gallons of lacquer, and the stands could hold 2,000 spectators for tournaments. From left to right, Stub Bubon, Woody Woodhame, Tom Blaylock, Eldon Martin, and Bob Solomon, comprising a local automobile dealer's bowling team, pose for a photographer. Below, a sign on the back wall thanks bowlers in 1994, the year Celebrity closed. (Right, David Forsyth collection; below, Roger Whitacre collection.)

CELEBRITY PINBALL ARCADE AND SHOOTING GALLERY, C. 1972. Arcade games were part of the Celebrity experience from the beginning. Pinball machines (above) and Skee-Ball, along with a shooting gallery (below) and a massive slot-car track, dominated the game rooms in the early days, but in the 1970s, management began to add newly invented video games, which eventually came to dominate players' attention. The center's new owners after 1979 added two additional rooms for games, increasing the number of machines to 300, along with billiard tables. (Both, David Forsyth collection.)

CELEBRITY LOUNGE CROWD, 1961. Foodservice and live entertainment was another major component of Celebrity Sports Center. Here, a crowd waits by a wall of Colorado field rock (chosen by the center's architects, Powers, Daly, DeRoss of Long Beach, California) to enter the white-tablecloth Celebrity Room and Lounge. Inside, diners encountered a similar rock wall, dramatically illuminated with recessed lighting, and a circular fireplace. (David Forsyth collection.)

CELEBRITY PUB, C. 1969. For a more casual experience, Celebrity offered a soda and snack bar for teens, and this "Hofbrau," a family pub with "barrel booths" and windows overlooking the swimming pool. Despite its popularity, Celebrity began to lose money in the early 1990s and closed on June 15, 1994. The 122,600-square-foot center was demolished in 1995 for a retail development. (David Forsyth collection.)

COUNTRY DINNER PLAYHOUSE, C. 1975 (ABOVE) AND 1990 (BELOW). After enjoying a Dallas dinner theater, Denver businessman Sam Newton, with friends Bob and Mary Boren, decided Denver needed one too. The 470-seat Country Dinner Playhouse opened on Clinton Street south of Arapahoe Road in 1970. Multitalented Bill McHale produced, directed, and starred in many shows, and performed in the round on a hydraulically descending stage (below; man unidentified). Preshow musical entertainment came from the Barnstormers (who doubled as waiters), a group with actors Lee Horsley, Morgan Fairchild, and Ted Shackelford among its alumni. Other actors who performed at the playhouse early in their careers include Amy Adams, Annaleigh Ashford, and Rachel deBenedet. In May 2007, actors arriving at the financially troubled theater found padlocked doors but performed *Evita* in the parking lot anyway. It was demolished in 2011. (Above, author's collection; below, DPL.)

CINDERELLA CITY, 1968. Engineer/developer Gerri Von Frellick worked for years to create Cinderella City, billed as America's largest shopping mall when it opened in 1968 (other malls elsewhere soon eclipsed it). Initially slated for a controversial site near Hampden Avenue and University Boulevard, the center was ultimately built where Englewood City Park had been, on Hampden Avenue near Santa Fe Drive. Its unusual W layout (above) allowed space for four department stores and 265 shops. The center's central point was the fountain in the Blue Room (below), from which the Blue, Gold, Rose, and Shamrock Malls branched. On the lower level, shoppers enjoyed Cinder Alley, a collection of tiny shops, some operated by artisans. After years of decline, which a 1983 renovation did not stem, the mall closed and was demolished in 1995. (Above, author's collection; below, DPL, X-8255.)

Visit us at
arcadiapublishing.com
··

CPSIA information can be obtained
at www.ICGtesting.com
Printed in the USA
LVHW100853040421
683371LV00040B/15